A Kharisma Exclusive

Love Thy Self

Kharisma

0

Love Thy Self
Workbook
Second Edition
Empowering Young Women of Color

ISBN# 9780981891521

This Workbook Includes:

Positive Affirmations, Famous Quotes,

Original Poetry and Beautiful Photography.

With a new appendix section!!!

Kharisma

Published by:

Miller Publishing & Consultation Services

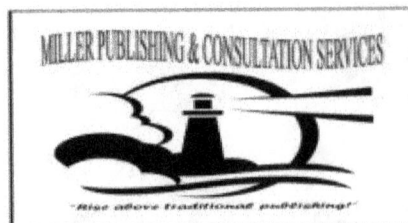

D.L. Miller@2011, 2023

freespiritenterprisesllc@gmail.com

Miller Publishing & Consultation Services

Richmond, VA

freespiritenterprises@gmail.com
Printed in the United States

Second Edition

ISBN 13: 978-0-9818915-2-1
ISBN 10: 0-9818915-2-7
LCCN: 2009912404

Editing: Miller Publishing & Consultation Services
Book Layout: Miller Publishing & Consultation
Services Cover Design: Tyron Arrington

In Dedication

I dedicate this book to my God daughters Stephanie and Melea; as well as all the other little girls, growing young ladies, and maturing women of the world, May every female reading this book inherit wisdom and self love that is overflowing.

-Kharisma

Acknowledgements

I must acknowledge God first. With Him all things are possible, and without Him none of this would have been possible. I also want to thank my family most of all, my mom, dad, and sister who have always supported me in everything I do, (even if they did not approve.)

My closest friends, Keisha, Rod, Oliver, and Sharlene were very encouraging and therefore assisted in the development of this book. My friend, Alesha, actually inspired the creation of the book. She asked me to write something positive and inspirational, as opposed to writing another drama-filled novel. Well this one's for you Alesha, but after this I go back to the drama! lol I also thank my co-workers and associates, especially those who supported my other work. I appreciate you for everything you do. Special thanks go out to my close, long time friend, aka "Suzie" who shared her personal story of trials and tribulations to help others who are going through a similar experience find the strength to move past their pain and find inner peace.

I thank my fans because you have been the reason I continue my mission of writing for the public. Otherwise, I would only be writing for myself. I hope this book inspires and motivates you all to reach your fullest potential.

-Kharisma

Table of Contents

<u>Introduction:</u>

The purpose of my writing

Many readers who happen to pick up this book may ask why I would choose to write it with an already large array of other self help materials collecting dust on the bookshelves. Well, with my perusal of the bookstores and libraries, I have found very few books written to address the self esteem issues of women, specifically women of color, and the great need for these women to celebrate self love and self preservation.

The mission of this book is to allow African-American, Latin American, and other American women of color the opportunity to embrace their individuality above societal norms, cultural expectations, gender roles, or any other forms of classism. Though we all fit into specific groups according to race, culture, and class, we women all collectively have something special, which makes us uniquely beautiful.

One may also ask why I would target women of color as opposed to speaking to women of all ethnic groups. One good reason to mention is the fact that I am an African-American woman who has enjoyed the journey of self discovery; its twists and turns, ups and downs, and all of its ins and outs. Despite all the obvious obstacles I have had as an African-American woman, I have learned to love who I am and achieve success with great pride. Secondly, I write to hopefully encourage and empower women of color to love themselves from the depths of their souls to the surface of their mahogany, honey-brown, or caramel skin. As beautiful as we are, collectively we have some serious issues with self esteem and confidence. Thirdly, I pray that this book will help women of color raise their little girls to love who they are, denying themselves for no one.

Peace and Blessings,

-Kharisma

Chapter 1

Accepting One Self

"There is no greater love than the love you discover from deep within your soul."- Kharisma

Accepting one self: What does that really mean? Does it mean to deny others for the greater purpose of individuality? Does it mean separating yourself from the groups for which you belong? Does it mean selfishly focusing on your needs, ignoring the needs of others? Well I guess my answer would be…yes and no. Self acceptance is a balance of loving yourself and giving yourself to others. You see, without self acceptance, you can not be of any service to others. The old adage is true: "To love others, you must first learn to love yourself." Most importantly, how can you find the beauty in others, when you can not find beauty in yourself?

In a perfect world, the first person you would fall in love with would be you, then family and friends, and finally your significant other. However, in the real world you know the order is quite different. Usually, as a little girl, you fall for your dad first, (if he's there,) then the rest of your family, friends, your significant other, and then if you have time left in your life from loving everyone else, you finally learn to love yourself. How crazy is that? I mean really. How often do you hear of people, (maybe even people like you,) who love their husband or boyfriend more than they love themselves? Accepting all kinds of abuse, emotional neglect, and mistreatment, all the while hoping for some sort of love in return. Ultimately, it is never returned. How can a person love you when you don't love yourself enough to reject abuse/mistreatment?

> *"Someone was hurt before you; wronged before you; hungry before you; frightened before you; beaten before you; humiliated before you; raped before you; yet someone survived." - Maya Angelou*

Surviving and Loving Yourself Beyond the Abuse

Whether it be domestic abuse, substance abuse, physical abuse or emotional abuse, whether the perpetrator is your husband, mother, sister, or even you; abuse is abuse, and it's just wrong. Accepting abuse means denying yourself of true happiness, and everyone deserves true happiness.

When one does not respect him or herself, one can easily fall prey to promiscuous behaviors, substance/alcohol abuse, depression, or even suicidal behavior. "When self respect takes its rightful place in the psyche, you will not allow yourself to be manipulated by anyone." (Indira Mahindra) It can hinder job opportunities, relationships, personal achievements, etc. For this reason, one must recognize a self destructive cycle or pattern before damaging effects occur.

"Suzie's Story"

(Based on true events, names changed to protect identities)

Suzie had been a friend of Kiara since high school. She was always a lot of fun and had the ability to make Kiara laugh every time she saw her. Suzie's spirit was positive and free until she started dating a man named Demond. He worked hard to destroy and conquer Suzie's spirit.

Suzie and Demond dated on and off for several years in a whirlwind of total confusion. Demond was able to win her over with his charm and sex appeal. He even befriended her closest friend, Kiara. The three of them would hang out together quite frequently. One day Suzie and Kiara headed to Demond's job to pick-up keys for the apartment. Demond apparently did not like the visit to his job as he proceeded to force Suzie to the ground, twisting her arms and yelling out curses. Kiara intervened by telling Demond to release Suzie. He continued hurting Suzie so Kiara hit Demond to help free her friend from harm. It was only a matter of time before Demond's rage turned on Kiara as well. So she bolted with her friend to the car. Demond attempted to punch through the glass window but was stopped in his tracks when the job supervisor screamed out the words, "you're fired."

Kiara just knew that Suzie would leave Demond alone for good after this incident in order to escape his mental and physical abuse. However, Suzie continued to date Demond, and Kiara and Suzie drifted further apart. Years later Kiara learned that Demond broke Suzie's arm. Suzie then finally said "enough is enough." Soon after the relationship was over, Suzie was able to move on to another man who helped her move passed her pain and actually experience joy in a relationship. She also strengthened her relationship with God which was the most powerful, causing her to look deep inside herself and appreciate the beautiful spirit she kept hidden during that painful part of her life.

9

Self Check

1) Have you ever experienced physical and/or emotional abuse like Suzie? If so, have you ever been able to move past the destructive cycle of abuse? How were you able to move past it? If it helps, write below about your experience.

_____

_____

_____

_____

_____

_____

_____

2) If you have not been abused, why do you think you have been able to avoid abusive situations/relationships?

_____

_____

_____

_____

_____

_____

3) What can be done to avoid potential abuse in the future?

_____

_____

_____

_____

_____

_____

When you look in the mirror, do you like what you see?
(Inside and Out?)

Why or Why Not?

_____

_____

_____

_____

_____

_____

_____

_____

Beautiful Flower

I love you Beautiful Flower, because you are who you are.
Though the strong winds blow through your petals threatening
you harm, you continue to grow and flourish each day.
The rain may pound you to the ground in May,
but as June arrived, you sprouted up and out
searching for the vibrant sun and blue skies above.
You gave off the most sweet aroma and colorful hues,
for which I have learned to appreciate.
I long to hold on to you forever,
but you continue to become lost
where I can not find you.
Each day I search for any essence of you.
Each day I feel somewhat hopeless we will be connected
Beautiful Flower, we will be one once again.
I know because you are my inseparable friend.
<In the name of self-love>

-Kharisma

12

I believe Iyanla Vanzant says it best: "The stress began the day you learned you were expected to please other people. Parents wanted you to be clean and quiet....Neighbors wanted you to be respectful and helpful.... whenever you failed to do exactly what someone expected of you, you weren't good, or good enough. You were bad, weak, or dumb. Unfortunately, you began to believe it. Giving in to the demands, day by day, you lost a little more of yourself and your understanding of the truth..."

- Vanzant, 1993

Putting on a "Mask of Confidence"

As women of color, especially women of African descent, we are automatically viewed as strong, independent women. We can withstand single motherhood, climb the career ladder, and explore our educational needs- all at the same time! Unknown to the world and ourselves, we have great pain hidden behind the mask. We feel we must conceal it, because we must not show signs of weakness. We must always exude confidence even when we are hurting on the inside. This is the BELIEF!

What's Behind Your Mask?

(Write a journal entry based on what you have been
hiding behind the mask to protect your image.)

_____

_____

_____

_____

_____

In order to accept oneself, we must learn:
The "Essential Keys."

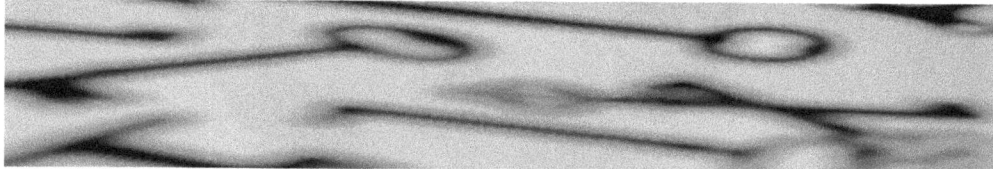

1.　　Realize your strengths and your weaknesses

2.　　Learn to embrace your differences

3.　　Live by all of your decisions

4.　　Move past the obstacles you have placed before your own path

5.　　Forgive yourself for your mistakes and learn from them

These keys may be difficult to execute at first. This is especially true since many women are programmed from birth to take care of others before caring for themselves. Many of us were taught as young girls to stand by the man in our lives and allow him to make the important decisions. Men are the leaders and women are the followers, right? This archaic belief system is as old as time itself and assumed by both men and women, even today. Nonetheless, there have always been many strong women in history who ensured that we have more equal rights and fair treatment than the generation before; Sojourner Truth, Harriet Tubman, Rosa Parks, and now our first lady, Michelle Obama- only to name a few. All of these women I imagine possess similar personality traits, such as confidence, leadership abilities, high self esteem, perseverance, and determination. As women of color, we must build up ourselves in order to help contribute to society. How do we accomplish this with so many obstacles in our way?

✔ **Expect and command respect from yourself and others.**
✔ **Treat yourself daily with something you love like a warm bath, enjoy your favorite food, or take part in some other fun activity.**
✔ **Honor self for all accomplishments, big and small.**
✔ **View life with a positive outlook using positive affirmations, meditations, and/or prayer daily.**

Practice the following relaxation exercises daily, (preferably in the morning for a lasting effect throughout the day.)

Deep Breathing Technique
(at least 2-3 minutes)

☐ Find a comfortable environment to meditate, (i.e. a quiet bedroom, bathroom, etc.)

☐ Switch off the light and block out any background noise/distractions

☐ Sit or lay in a relaxed position

☐ Close your eyes

☐ Take in a few deep breaths

    1. Inhale air for 2-3 seconds

    2. Hold for 2-3 seconds

    3. Exhale air for 2-3 seconds

    4. Repeat at least 3 more times

Tense and Relax Technique
(at least 2-3 minutes)

Directly following the deep breathing technique, start relax and tense technique:

    1. Tighten both fists simultaneously

    2. Release both fists simultaneously

    3. Repeat 3 more times

    4. Tighten both feet simultaneously

    5. Release both feet simultaneously

    6. Repeat 3 more times

***Now you can move into the meditation exercise,
(you may prefer to sit or lay on a mat.)***

Meditation 1 - Beach Scene

(10 - 20 minutes)

You are far, far away in the most beautiful place you have ever been in your life. A paradise, if you will. Imagine a place of comfort like a beach or park. This is your special little place where no one can bother you. You can block out the stress and negative auras from your day because you are miles away from work or school, and the hustle and bustle of normal life. It is so nice to be able to retreat and clear your mind of clutter.

You are allowed to think happy thoughts, taking in the calming environment around you. Maybe you smell fresh flowers in a garden or the salty air of the beach. You may hear the beautiful sounds like birds chirping or the sounds of ocean waves crashing upon the shore. You can see the sunrise above the horizon and all its pretty colors dancing across the sky. The soft breeze whispers sweet words in your ear. You can even feel the sun kiss your skin. The warmth feels so nice and relaxing that you drift off to sleep. And you dream....

Meditation 2 - Mountain Scene
(10 - 20 minutes)

As you slowly close your eyes, you are quickly transported to a different place. A remote area with powerful mountains cascading with snow, cool mountain streams, and clear, brisk skies above. You are surrounded by nothing but nature, the hustle and bustle of life has vanished with the blink of an eye. The air is cool and clear. You hear nothing but birds singing soft songs in the background. You feel more refreshed than ever before.

Free to think what you want to think and feel what you want to feel, you are now compelled to dream....

Chapter 2

Individuality

"With all my imperfections, I love being me!"- Kharisma

Times have changed from the days of the fifties, (before I was born by the way,) to the late nineties, and now the new millennium. From a time when women were often expected to cater to men, denying themselves as individuals to a new day of feminism and independence.

> "Without individuality in today's society, the world would be filled with a population of large numbers of followers as opposed to leaders." –oppaper.com

Knowing I was different and sort of an outcast, I learned at a very young age to embrace who I was as an individual. I realized even though I had few friends and associates to connect with, I could truly depend on one person to be there for me for always, and that person was me. Being my own person apart from everyone in my circle gave me a feeling of empowerment. Though at times, I went through bouts of feeling lonely, rejected, and even depressed, my inner spirit brought me out of the mess I was in and into a whole new world.

Suddenly, I began to do things like going to the movies alone and actually enjoying the experience! I had become so tired of waiting for a friend to take time out or get the opportunity to go out with me. The excuses, as you can imagine, became repetitive and I grew tired of hearing them. "Oh...um, I gotta get a babysitter first and we'll see" or "I...uh...don't have money to do it this week, maybe next week." or the most infamous excuse, "I gotta wash my hair tonight, let's see about tomorrow." Guess what? Tomorrow would never come. So there I sat, at home, wishing I could go to the movies, but I couldn't because I had no one to join me. Then I asked myself, "Why not go to the movies anyway?" Since I had no excuse for myself, I decided to have an official date- with myself! I found that I had more fun dating myself, (most times,) than dating other people. It may sound pathetic or strange to some, but it really isn't. In this scenario, I had no one to negotiate with regarding the activity, no need to make arrangements to meet or pick someone up, and most of all, I had no one to appease but myself. How refreshing is it to not have to impress the person on the date, because your date loves everything you love, you agree on everything, you have the same personality, and the same beautiful face. Don't get me wrong, I enjoy the company of my close friends and family, but once in a while I prefer to do things alone, independent of others.

<u>**Ask yourself**</u>: Have I missed out on a lot of fun things in my life because I was afraid my loved ones may not approve? Have people successfully discouraged me from doing what I wanted to do? Have I missed out on a lot because I had no one to accompany me on outings? Have I sat at home numerous times waiting for someone, anyone to go out with me? Have I constantly questioned people about my life before making decisions for my life? If your answer is "yes" to any of these questions, you must ask yourself "why?" And then ask yourself "Why not?" as in "Why not do what I want to do with my own life?"

Why not experience the life you want to live? Why not make your dreams come true? Why not reach the goals you want to achieve? Why not become the person you were meant to be without the interference of others?

Write these thoughts below:

_____

_____

_____

_____

_____

_____

As an individual, you have the opportunity to make your own choices, find your own way, and be your own person. Being an individual makes one accountable for his/her actions. Hence, the ultimate say, (regarding your life,) is yours. Not your mother, not your best friend, and even the Almighty God gives you the free will to make choices for yourself. Although we may not have complete control of our circumstances or the world around us, we all have control over the decisions we make. Free will is a beautiful thing and we as individuals must use it to decide what path we should take in life. Whether you turn left, right, keep straight ahead, or just stand still, never turn back. You can not undo the journey traveled. Many of us at times (including myself) may stay stuck in the past. We believe that if it was a great past, it may help us cope with the perceived dreadful present or future ahead. However, if the past was awful, we may stay stuck there, because we do not know how to move past the pain and hurt to enjoy a much better present and more hopeful future. Sometimes, living in a painful place is more comfortable than experiencing something new and unfamiliar. We must realize we as individuals have complete control over this kind of unhealthy mentality and so being miserable for an extended period of time is your choice.

From the moment you take your first breath to the moment you take your last, you will and have always had the ultimate say on what you do with your life. Though as a child, you may have been heavily influenced by your family, friends, co-workers, and associates, as an adult, it's up to you how much of a role they play in your life.

In the great words of Pearl Bailey, "You can not belong to anyone else until you belong to yourself." I empower you to embrace your own uniqueness and differences as opposed to embracing what is special about someone else. You are who you are and will never be the person you idolize. Be part of the group, but still be you. All of the values, morals, interests you had coming into the group situation, leave with them, plus the positive impressions of the group. In turn, make a positive impression on others that they can take with them, but you must still keep a balance between social conformity and individuality, making sure not to lose who you are when meshing with society, a group dynamic or partnership.

Chapter 3
Standing Out in a Crowd

"Nothing comes to dreamers, but a dream..." - Unknown

Of all the nations in the world, America is a nation that embraces individuality and standing out amongst the crowd the most. However, as we all know, America is full of contradictions since its citizens often seek to blend in with or hide behind the crowd. Following social norms and being accepted, often overshadows individuality.

Author and poet, Erica Jong states, "It takes courage to lead a life. Any life." However, many times, it is safer and more comfortable to follow the leader, placing great expectations and responsibility on the shoulders of others. As the leader, you are not only responsible for what other people say and do, but also how you influence what they say and do. It takes a significant amount of courage and charisma to influence others, whether good or bad. Being a leader or a follower usually comes naturally, often apparent at a very young age. This was especially true for me since my parents saw the traits of a leader very early on. I was a loner, different from other children, and quite independent. Although I had supportive parents, I often needed to rely upon myself to make and carry through decisions. Of course, this could be a serious problem for a young child to so called "buck the system" or rebel against the rules. I didn't go too far outside the boundary lines, but certainly if I didn't agree with what I was being told I let it be known. I questioned authority and rules. When I felt the rules did not make sense or were unfair, I refused to comply, regardless of the punishment or consequences. All in all I was viewed as the quiet, good girl who usually did what was right, but it was always based on her terms, never theirs.

Being a natural-born leader has its ups and downs. I have had a long list of personal accomplishments over my lifetime, which has made me feel proud. Nonetheless, I have also had a lot of let downs associated with failing to meet the high standards and expectations of my parents as well as my own. Put all those components together and you have a lot of stress and pressure. Was it all worth it? If you ask me, hell yeah! Regardless of the pressure, being a strong individual has made me feel important, motivated, and purposeful. We leaders are doers and thinkers, not dreamers. Though it is great to dream, those dreams can become reality if you can only push pass the dream. A Sri Lankan scholar, Bawa Muhaiyaddeen, states: "In the solitude of your mind are the answers to all your questions about your life. You must take time to ask and listen." Relaxing for long periods of time and doing nothing is so over rated. Be sure that while your friends and associates are busy "chilling out," you are busy getting things done. Achieve what you want and need for your life, with a strong will and determination anything is possible. According to Ashanti proverbs, "You must act as if it is impossible to fail." (Vanzant, 1993) Nothing could be closer to the truth.

She Stuck Out Like a Sore Thumb

Amongst others, she was so odd. So uncool. Just not what's happening. In a world where being unique is ugly and being different was making a choice to be detached from the rest of the world. An outcast to join other dreads of society or be banished to be alone with herself. From the darkness, she found her light. Deep within her soul. She learned to love her weird little intricacies. All of the finely woven pieces, making up her colorful personality. What a beauty to behold, so uniquely made! Like no other. She is God's gift to the world. Will you take her for granted?

-Kharisma

Standing out in the crowd is not an easy or comfortable process. Trust me, I know from personal experience. It has its downfalls, whether it comes naturally or it's something you are trying to achieve. At times, finding yourself alone, carrying the weight of the world on your shoulders. Other times, feeling misunderstood and unaccepted. But I have found with self acceptance comes self love and with self love comes love and appreciation from others. They will eventually learn to see your special light that shines from within. You must not dim your light to camouflage yourself with the masses, instead shine it brighter for all to see.

What makes you stand out apart from your family, friends, or co-workers/classmates?

1._____

2._____

3._____

4._____

5._____

6._____

Chapter 4
Being Accepted without Denying One Self

"Change yourself for no one, unless that someone is you." –Kharisma

To be honest and true, most people, including myself strive to be accepted by other people. No matter how self-sufficient and independent we may be, we all need to feel like we are loved and like we are part of something bigger than ourselves.

Since it is unhealthy to fall too far to the extremes of being totally alone or totally enmeshed with others, how do you maintain a healthy balance? Well, I must say, this process is complex, since we all have different experiences and personalities. One may fluctuate from being a social butterfly and back to being a loner depending on what he/ she has been through in his/her life. For example, a traumatic experience like death in the family can send a social person into a deep depression. This is a situation which could result in the person becoming withdrawn and alone. By the same token, an uplifting experience like a graduation or wedding can cause a loner to come out of his/her shell and explore the world for all it has to offer.

In my opinion, it is always best to fall somewhere in the middle of being a loner and being socially enmeshed, being careful not to fall too far to one extreme or the other. To maintain a healthy sense of self and the outside would at the same time is essential. Unfortunately, many of us get lost, either not knowing where we fit in the grand scheme of things or not knowing who we are. For this reason, it is so important to evaluate ourselves on a regular basis, monitoring where we fall on the continuum of sociability.

Where do you fall in the social continuum?

- Reclusive
    - 0-3 Rating
    - Does not partake in social activities. Stays to him/ herself most of the time if not all of the time.

- Social-Personal Balance
    - 4-7 Rating
    - Participates in social activities on a regular basis (2-3 x's per week), however makes time for personal activities as well.

- Socially Enmeshed
    - 8-10 Rating
    - Is often if not always involved in social activities, does not make time to be to him/herself often. Feels uncomfortable being alone.

In your evaluation of yourself, if you found that you fell too far to the left of the continuum, I would recommend you seek the acceptance of others by becoming more social. Join a club or special interest group in order to meet people like yourself. Enjoy meeting new individuals and having new experiences in your life. The people who are usually outgoing and popular will like you, because you are more laid back and grounded. You take time to smell the roses and you know exactly who you are as a person and they envy that about you. Assist the social butterfly with becoming more connected to their inner being, more comfortable with who they are on the inside.

If you feel you gravitated too far to the right, my suggestion would be to spend more time getting to know the person who dwells within you. Take time for self evaluation and reflection. Figure out what makes YOU happy, not your friends, church members, family, or co-workers. Think about your dreams and aspirations and figure out how to make each one of them come to fruition-one seedling at a time. As a social butterfly, people are naturally drawn to you. You will not have to work hard to get people to like you. They already do. The individuals who are usually shy and quiet enjoy your company, because you are more exciting and adventurous. Help them be more comfortable with group situations, and invite them to blossom in the social world as you already have.

In the next section, there is a brainstorming map activity which can be used to help you to explore your connection with the world; implementing changes to achieve your desired effect. A sample map has been filled in for you as well.

Your brainstorm can branch off as far as you need it to branch off. The purpose of the activity is to set goals in order to change your life the way you would like it to be. You may even want to give yourself time restraints or deadlines to make those things happen in your life.

***Note how specific the objectives are listed in each goal area referring to time of day, how frequent the goal will be addressed, etc.

Use this space to create a map of your goals and small steps towards your goals:

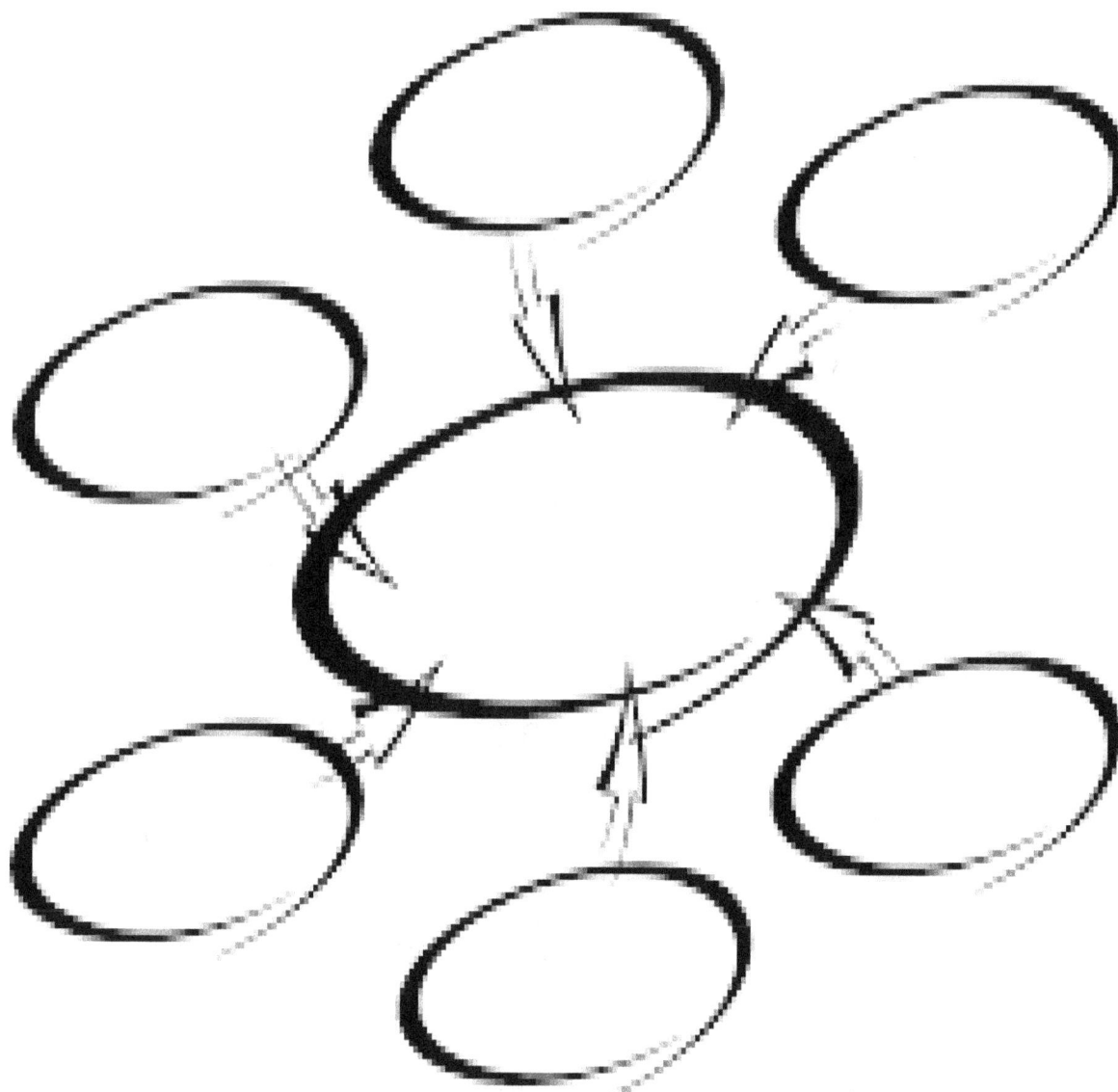

Your Self Image

Do you worry about how other people perceive you? Based on the measuring stick of society, do you feel like you are not good enough to be accepted and loved by others? Too skinny? Too fat? Too tall? Too short? Too quiet? Too loud? Not fun enough? Not interesting enough? Not good enough? Just not good enough? Most of us are unaware that we have issues of self esteem. We tell ourselves how great we are and rationalize that others should love us too. But deep down below our subconscious, we really have some serious hang-ups connected to our background, traumatic experiences, negative associations with other people, etc. Often these hang-ups and past hurts cause us to become defensive thus building an imaginary wall between ourselves and other people.

Self Image Inventory

I. How do you view yourself? (Check all that apply below)

-Attractive -Annoying -Respectful -Intelligent

-Humorous -Impatient -Honest -Irritable -Bossy

- Lonely -Inventive -Timid -Cheerful -Shallow -

Personable -Charming -Naïve - Free-Spirit

- _____

- _____

- _____

- _____

II. How do you think others view you? (Check all that apply below) -Sweet -Shy -Quiet -Moody -Angry -Bright

-Dramatic -Versatile -Boring -Full of life -Pleasant

-Motivated -Fashionable -Arrogant -Persuasive

-Closed-Minded -Genuine -Giving

- _____

- _____

- _____

- _____

Looking back at your evaluation, did you have more positives than negatives overall? Were more of the negatives found in the second section versus the first? Would your answers have changed had you completed the inventory on another day? Hopefully, this inventory helped provide you a vivid picture of how you perceive yourself in relation to other people.

If you had more positives than negatives in both sections, it signifies a healthy self image. However, if you had a lot of positives in Section I and a lot of negatives in Section II, then one can conclude that you have (what I call,) "the world is against me" complex. I am a great person, but I don't know why people don't like me. In this case, you are using defense mechanisms to protect your fragile ego. You really do not feel good about yourself, but you are going to defend yourself at all cost.

If you had a lot of negatives in both Section I and Section II, then one can conclude that you have (what I call,) "I am not worthy" complex. I am not a good person and I don't like myself. Therefore, others don't like me either. In this case, you probably have some serious issues to work out from the inside that are projecting out to others.

If you had more positives in Section II than Section I, then one can conclude that you have (what I call), "the self-defeating complex." I am not worthy of love but people feel sorry for me and they feel obligated to do and say nice things. In this case, you can not see how special of a person you really are, but everyone around you does and you can't believe it. You are so used to dwelling in self pity and putting yourself down that you can't receive the love others try to relay to you.

Many times self image problems require professional counseling to help undo past psychological or emotional damage. However, self evaluation is a healthy start to your emotional recovery.

Phenomenal Woman

Pretty women wonder where my secret lies.
I'm not cute or built to suit a fashion model's size.
But when I start to tell them, They think I'm telling lies.
I say,

It's in the reach of my arms
The span of my hips,
The stride of my step,
The curl of my lips.
I'm a woman
Phenomenally.
Phenomenal woman,
That's me. I walk into a room
Just as cool as you please,
And to a man,
The fellows stand or
Fall down on their knees.
Then they swarm around me,
A hive of honey bees.
I say,
It's the fire in my eyes,
And the flash of my teeth,
The swing in my waist,
And the joy in my feet.
I'm a woman
Phenomenally.
Phenomenal woman,
That's me.

Phenomenal Woman cont…

Men themselves have wondered
What they see in me.
They try so much
But they can't touch
My inner mystery.
When I try to show them,
They say they still can't see.
I say,
It's in the arch of my back,
The sun of my smile,
The rise of my breasts,
The grace of my style.
…I'm a woman
Phenomenally.
Phenomenal woman,
That's me.
Now you understand
Just why my head's not bowed.
I don't shout or jump about
Or have to talk real loud.
When you see me passing
It ought to make you proud.
I say,
It's in the click of my heels,
The bend of my hair,
The palm of my hand,
The need for my care,
'Cause I'm a woman
Phenomenally.
Phenomenal woman,
That's me.
© **Maya Angelou, 1978.**

Chapter 5

The Colors of the Rainbow: The Uniqueness of Others
"Natural beauty comes in all colors, strength in many forms. When we learn to honor the differences and appreciate the mix, we're in harmony." - Unknown

With accepting yourself of course it is only fair to accept the differences which lie within others. In turn, in order to achieve the love and acceptance of others you must accept their differences, intricacies, and yes, even their flaws must appear to be beautiful because they are, just like your flaws. They are what make an individual unique and interesting. God designed it that way, well at least that is how I feel we were designed.

Below is a self evaluation form that allows you to be honest with yourself.

I really do not like people who_____

_____

_____

It is difficult for me to accept….

_____

_____

_____

I think _____ is interesting but is too weird for me
to try.

Why do _____ people usually_____?

Why don't _____ people rarely

_____

_____

_____?

So what do you think? Did you shock yourself with how intolerant you were of people who did not share your type of lifestyle, beliefs, attitudes, or background? Maybe even a little prejudice- just a little? Those traits lie within all of us, because we are all human. Everyone has judged someone else in their lifetime, (Yes, I am guilty again of that one.) But it is important to understand how stereotyping and close-minded thinking can block your connections with some really good people.

I empower you to go out one day, maybe a free day you have off from work or after work, and find a place that is bustling with people, (i.e., a park or mall,) and just watch. Watch with a different eye than before. Look for the most unique person you can find or maybe a person who is perceived a certain way, because of his "thug wear" or her "nappy locs" or "their alternative lifestyle." Block out your usual internal dialogue in order to relate to them and imagine yourself having a conversation. Hell, venture out and actually talk with them. That's if they are not too scary for you. Ask questions and get to know the person inside. There is an old adage, "It's not the book's cover that matters, but what lies within its pages." I believe this is true. Our outer shell is actually only a shell, only there for appearances. Our inner mass is who we truly are, what many do not see until they actually get to know us. Character, values, beliefs, and personality are beneath our outer shell. For some individuals their shells may be very thin revealing the inner soul inside. For others the shell may be thick and opaque, and hard to penetrate to their soul. This is especially true when people are hurt, mistreated, or deceived, usually resulting in major trust issues. The tough outer shell serves as protection against further emotional harm. Unfortunately, this causes a block in communication with others causing a deterioration of relationships or preventing the formation of relationships in the first place. This is when self healing is in order.

Do You Need Self Healing?

0-5 scale: 0-not at all – 5-All the time)

Have trouble leaving behind past hurts? _____

Accuse new people of being guilty of other people's past behaviors? _____

Have difficulty maintaining stable relationships with others? _____

Do you assume people will cause you harm before you even get to know them? _____

 Have thoughts of "getting them" before they can "get you?" _____

Have a hard time believing what people tell you? _____

Need an extended amount of time to get over a broken relationship? _____

Do you carry a lot of "emotional baggage," which tends to make you resentful/bitter?

_____

Self Healing Evaluation

*If you scored more than 3 "5's", you definitely need self healing and should possibly consider a support group, therapy, or spiritual counseling.

*If you scored 3 "5's", you need some self healing which can include meditation, prayer, journaling, etc.

*If you scored 2 or less "5's", you have some minor issues with building trust. You may be able to "heal" yourself with more social interaction and relationship building.

*If you found that you only have some moderate issues, (mostly 1's and 2's), the most important thing to do is to make sure these issues do not worsen over time. That is why it is important to evaluate yourself honestly and frequently.

*If you have little to no issues then be thankful and careful to avoid a collection of baggage as life throws you curveballs and people do things that cause you pain.

Appreciation is essential in developing healthy connections with other people. Appreciating the people in your life creates deeper relationships. Some people may even say our actual life purpose is to be somehow linked to the people introduced to us in our lives. I am a firm believer that each and every person we come in contact with is there for a specific reason. Even those short "chance" meetings which may occur on the bus ride to work or inside the mall while shopping or at the laundromat while washing clothes. Those who stay for the "seasons" of our lives are possibly there only to provide us support, teach us a lesson, or protect us from certain circumstances.

I have personally had relationships with people that lasted an extended period of time and for some unknown reason it gradually diminished. It's like, "There you see 'um and now you don't." This occurrence used to leave me feeling confused, hurt, and unloved. But as I grew in my age and hopefully wisdom, I learned that those "ghost" relationships were there for a reason. Either I gained something from the other party or they gained something from me or it was a mutual need that was fulfilled between us. I believe God uses us as tools to bring about His purpose. So for instance, if you needed someone to help you get over a failed relationship, he may send a person into your life to fill the void or provide emotional support until you are strong enough to move past the hump. Knowing this causes us to appreciate the individuals who are there for whatever reason and vice-versa. Unbeknownst to some of us, we are there to help realize a need for someone else. If we are there fulfilling a need and we are aware we are there for that specific reason, we usually expect to be appreciated for what we have done. Whether we admit it or not, we need to feel validated, purposeful, and needed.

A World Without Me

A world without me is a world with one less beautiful smile and minus two sparkling eyes of wonder.

A world with one less unique style and lovely personality.

A world with less motivation, determination, and perseverance.

A world without me is a world with not enough spice and flavor. With such a vest for life and love for self and others, I am an inspiration to all that know me.

-Kharisma

I can't imagine a world without my existence. What about you? Now just close your eyes and imagine for a moment a world without you. How would it be? I know what you may be thinking, "The world would have gone on without me as usual." But that is so untrue. Think about how the world wouldn't have been touched, influenced, or affected by your spirit, if you would have never existed. If you have children, they would have never been born either and their lives would have never been touched by you. Nor could they touch the lives of others for that matter. If you are married, your husband would have never been able to meet his soul mate. Your parents would have never been able to experience the joy of having such a unique child as yourself. Your community and jobsite would have never been blessed with your special gifts and talent. The day you were born you changed the world and you will leave your personal mark until the day you die.

Now that you realize the depth of your existence in this world, you can write your own self-inspired poem on the next page.

A world without me…

_____

_____

_____

_____

_____

_____

_____

_____

_____

_____

~ _____

Chapter 6
The Journey to Inner Peace, Love, and Happiness
**"The path to a peaceful life may be short or long,
but one must stay the course to achieve it." ~Kharisma**

~~~~~~~~~~~~~~~~~~

Peace

~~~~~~~~~~~~~~~~~~

According to the late, great Marvin Gaye, "If you can not find peace within yourself, you will never find it anywhere else." Wise words, but how does one achieve inner peace? Does one achieve it through religion? Self reflection? Personal trials and tribulations? A journey around the world? Or maybe a retreat away from everyone and everything? Does it take a lifetime of lessons to achieve inner peace or is it the time it takes to achieve the wisdom required to be at peace? Do only spiritual gurus like Gandhi and Mother Teresa find peace or is it achievable by any man or woman who has his/her mind and heart open to receive it?

I do not claim to be a philosopher, spiritual advisor, or even a religious person, but I believe everyone must find peace on his/her own accord. There is no one recipe for achieving a peaceful life, although I believe there are common ingredients to facilitate the process. These elements include:

- Love for self and others
- A spiritual connection with a higher power
- Holistic balance (mind, body and soul working together as a unit.)

Balancing these major components with so many other components of life, (i.e., finances, career, health, etc.,) are especially difficult. Once a person has achieved the components required for peace the other components usually fall into place. One must create a balance by strengthening the weak components and maintaining the strong ones. For example, if you have a good relationship with yourself, but you have a weak spiritual connection with your God, then you must take the steps to strengthen your spirituality.

John 14:27   Peace I leave with, my peace I give to you: not as the world giveth, give I unto you. Let not your heart be troubled, neither let it be afraid.

Personal Affirmations for Empowering Your Spirit:

❖ Enjoy life's journey steering straight ahead never looking back.

❖ Find your purpose and fulfill it as God would want it fulfilled.

❖ Trust in Him, though the road may become bumpy, you will make it to your destination.

❖ Know God first before you praise Him.

❖ Understand God in order to please Him.

My Personal Editorial of Religion & Spirituality

I am on a spiritual journey myself, still learning and connecting with God. One thing I know for sure is the importance of knowing your higher power before you get too caught up in the religious traditions and expectations. I believe it is best to develop a personal relationship with God first. I realize this is a touchy subject for many. You may disagree with my beliefs, especially if you are heavily involved in the church. But I think all can agree that in order to praise your God you must first know who he is and thus your path should began with his teachings. The Holy Bible or the Koran or The Book of Latter Day Saints, whatever religious book represents your beliefs, it should be your foundation. The church may be the place where you have the teachings interpreted, but be careful who interprets them for you. Make sure that your religious leader has the spiritual food you need to survive spiritually and your church home should be just that...like your home. If you feel uncomfortable or unfulfilled, God may be sending you a message that the place you have chosen for spiritual guidance is not the place for you. Don't get me wrong, I do not believe that one should wander aimlessly looking for the right place, but he/she should trust that God will lead the way. "Seek and ye shall find" (Matthew 7:7) Another thing I stand firm on is the belief that people should help one another because it is what God wants us to do. There are some individuals who praise God but do not follow his teachings. I say unto you, we are placed on this Earth to do right by others not only to worship God and congregate in a church. Dr. Oscar Lane couldn't have said it better, "You can be so heavenly bound that you are no earthly good." Nothing could be truer than that statement. How can you spend several days a week attending church, praying and reading your holy book daily; only to step over the homeless, the poor, the misguided youth, the people with disabilities, and even your own family members who need your help? Not only does it not make spiritual sense, but that form of thinking lacks rational sense. Everyone on Earth has and will continue to need someone else's help, and in turn should step up to help others. This system of reciprocity was perfectly designed in that manner. I empower you to truly do God's work in your communities, your schools, your homes, everywhere you go.

~Kharisma

~~~~~~~~~~~~~~~~

Hope & Trust

~~~~~~~~~~~~~~~~

When all seems lost and all hope is gone, what do you do? Who can you turn to? Hopefully, you have family and good friends to lean on. But even if you do have supportive people in your corner, dealing with painful situations can be difficult. Death. Job loss. Broken relationships. Financial Woes. When the hard times last too long, it's easy to lose hope. You may feel helpless, like there is nothing or no one who can help you through your situation. For these times you must draw from your inner strength, your higher power, and in some cases you may need to seek professional help as mentioned earlier. There is counseling for just about every problem imaginable. If you have an issue which requires more than you have to give, don't hesitate to ask for help. Many times these spiritual counseling services are affordable and effective in resolving problems.

> **Psalm 18:2**
> *The Lord is my rock, and my fortress, and my deliverer; my God, my strength, in whom I will trust; my buckler, and the horn of my salvation, and my high tower.*

~~~~~~~~~~~~~~~

Strength

~~~~~~~~~~~~~~~

Of course it is easy for most to have strength during periods of success and prosperity. When everything is going smoothly, one can feel as though he/she is on top of the world. But how do you stay strong when everything in your world is crashing around you?

Inner strength is required to keep a person afloat. Oftentimes, people learn to deal with hardship when they have prior experience. The first time is the hardest, but as you experience trauma, you learn ways to cope and move on. You may need to lean on friends, family, and God for support when you're feeling weak.

> **Psalm 27**
> *The Lord is my light and my salvation, whom shall I fear? The Lord is the strength of my life; whom shall I be afraid? When the wicked, even mine enemies and my foes, came upon me to eat up my flesh, they stumbled and fell. Though a host should encamp against me, my heart shall not fear; though war should rise against me, in this will I be confident.*

~~~~~~~~~~~~~~

Support

~~~~~~~~~~~~~~

We must support one another to make the world go 'round. If everyone was only "out for self" then each individual would have a hard time making it. We get more things accomplished working together and helping each other out. "Pay it forward," to a friend, family member, or even a stranger, watch how it comes back around to you when you need it most.

Psalm 40
I waited patiently for the Lord; and he inclined unto me, and heard my cry. He brought me up also out of a horrible pit, out of the miry clay, and set my feet upon a rock, and established my goings.

~~~~~~~~~~~~~~~~~~~

Love & Happiness

~~~~~~~~~~~~~~~~~~~~

Love and happiness are two emotions most people hope to feel consistently throughout their lifetime. They are good and they make people happy. Unfortunately, in the world we live in today, it may seem that people thrive off hate and destruction with an increase of drugs, crime, and war, deceit, and backstabbing, selflessness and greed, divorce and dismantling of families. Negativity is all around. How do we get back to the days when love, peace, and happiness were actually cool? A time when people had love in their hearts and warmth in their souls. I believe it is still deep down in everyone on earth, but we must multiply love with good gestures and random acts of kindness.

John 15:11
These things have spoken unto you, that my joy might remain in you, and that your joy might be full.

What I am Thankful for:

_____

_____

_____

_____

_____

_____

_____

LOVE SELF

Live your life to the fullest with no regrets.

Observe negative patterns occurring in your life.

Visit people of wisdom as often as possible.

Express yourself to others with no apologies.

Secure who you are and don't let go.

Eliminate self defeating beliefs.

Love thy self and others.

Free yourself of pain, hurt, and defeat.

References

Angelou, Maya. (1978) Phenomenal Woman. Extracted from website: August 24, 2009. http://www.kalimunro.com/phenomenal_woman.html.

Angelou, Maya. Quoted by: Iyanla Vanzant. (1993). Acts of Faith: Daily Meditations For People of Color. Fireside, New York, New York, Simon and Schuster Inc.

Jong, Erica. Extracted from website: August 18, 2009. http://www.famousquotesandauthors.com/ authors/erica_jong_quotes.html.

Lane, Oscar. Quoted by: Iyanla Vanzant. (1993). Acts of Faith: Daily Meditations For People of Color. Fireside, New York, New York, Simon and Schuster Inc.

Mahindra, Indira. Quoted by: Iyanla Vanzant.. (1993). Acts of Faith: Daily Meditations For People of Color. Fireside, New York, New York, Simon and Schuster Inc.

Muhaiyaddeen, Bawa. Quoted by: Iyanla Vanzant.. (1993). Acts of Faith: Daily Meditations For People of Color. Fireside, New York, New York, Simon and Schuster Inc.

The Holy Bible: King James Version. (2003) Paradise Press Inc. Weston, Florida.

Unknown Author. Extracted from website:

July 17, 2009.

http://www.oppapers.com/essays/Conformity-Vs
Individuality/15112

Vanzant, Iyanla. (1993). Acts of Faith: Daily Meditations For People
of Color. Fireside, New York, New York, Simon and Schuster Inc.

Bonus Section

A. Pre-Evaluation:

Self Love Inventory

B. Miller Interest & Personality Inventory (MIPI)

C. Personal Affirmations

D. Journal of Weekly Progress

E. Post-Evaluation:

Self Love Inventory

F. Personal Notes

A. <u>Pre-Evaluation: Self Love Inventory</u> *(1-rarely true - 5-usually true)*

1. I have the ability to make my own decisions.   1 2 3 4 5

2. I accept my imperfections.   1 2 3 4 5

3. When I'm alone, I enjoy myself.   1 2 3 4 5

4. I know I am a good person with a lot of qualities people love.   1 2 3 4 5

5. It is easy for me to gain the acceptance of others.   1 2 3 4 5

6. I am pleased with who I am.   1 2 3 4 5

7. I do not allow people to disrespect or mistreat me.   1 2 3 4 5

8. I speak up when I feel I'm being treated unfairly by others.   1 2 3 4 5

9. I am pleased with where my life is headed.   1 2 3 4 5

10. When people criticize me, I listen to what they have to say, but I do not allow their comments to bring my self esteem down.   1 2 3 4 5

11. I believe I am unique and there is no one on earth like me.   1 2 3 4 5

12. I forgive myself for my past mistakes.   1 2 3 4 5

13. I feel needed and loved by others.   1 2 3 4 5

14. I have grown a lot from last year.   1 2 3 4 5

15. I can imagine myself being more successful in a year or two.   1 2 3 4 5

Miller Interest & Personality Inventory

*Indicate the best number for each question:

1-not at all, 2- a little, 3- sometimes, 4- often, a lot-5

_____ 1. I think about the future.

_____ 2. I feel loved. by others.

_____ 3. I wish I could be a better person.

_____ 4. My family is important to me.

_____ 5. People don't understand me.

_____ 6. I am a happy person.

_____ 7. I am a good student.

_____ 8. I admit when I'm wrong.

_____ 9. I enjoy learning.

_____ 10. It is hard to do new things.

_____ 11. I wish I could do math.

_____ 12. I feel supported by my parents.

_____ 13. I get so mad I hit things.

_____ 14. I can't seem to keep up w/my stuff.

_____ 15. I don't feel like doing anything.

_____ 16. I hate when people criticize me.

_____ 17. I wish I wasn't so sad.

_____ 18. My friends are good to me.

_____ 19. People just don't understand me.

_____ 20. I get blamed for everything.

_____ 21. Respect is earned not given.

_____ 22. I can't seem to stay in one place.

_____ 23. My mind wanders too much.

_____ 24. I can control myself when upset.

_____ 25. I chose to do what I want.

_____ 26. I have problems thinking ahead.

_____ 27. I love meeting new people.

_____ 28. I feel good about who I am.

_____ 29. It's hard to find good friends.

_____ 30. I don't let people bother me.

B. <u>Personal Daily Affirmations</u>
(Read aloud one affirmation each morning.)

✔ **Today is the day I will start making my dreams come true.**

✔ **Today, I will keep a positive outlook despite any negative forces in my life.**

✔ **Today, I will treat others with respect and I will in turn receive respect.**

✔ **Today, I will block negativity from the inside and the outside world.**

✔ **Today, I will allow my life to go in the direction it destined to go with no regrets.**

✔ **Today, I will lend a helping hand to someone else.**

✔ **Today will be my day to grow, learn, and flourish!**

C. Journal of Weekly Progress

Week 1

My target goal of the week:

_____

I will address this goal by:

1._____**2.**

_____**3.**_

_____**4.**__

_____**My**

progress towards this goal was:

How can I improve towards this goal area:

_____

_____

Week 2
My target goal of the week:

_____

I will address this goal by:

1._____

2._____

3._____

4._____

My progress towards this goal was:

How can I improve towards this goal area:

_____

_____

Week 3
My target goal of the week:

_____

I will address this goal by:

1._____

2._____

3._____

4._____

My progress towards this goal was:

How can I improve towards this goal area:

_____

_____

Week 4
My target goal of the week:

_____

I will address this goal by:

1._____

2._____

3._____

4._____

My progress towards this goal was:

How can I improve towards this goal area:

_____

_____

Week 5
My target goal of the week:

_____

I will address this goal by:

1._____

2._____

3._____

4._____

My progress towards this goal was:

How can I improve towards this goal area:

_____

_____

Week 6
My target goal of the week:

_____

I will address this goal by:

1._____

2._____

3._____

4._____

My progress towards this goal was:

How can I improve towards this goal area:

_____

_____

Week 7

My target goal of the week:

_____

I will address this goal by:

1._____

2._____

3._____

4._____

My progress towards this goal was:

How can I improve towards this goal area:

_____

_____

Week 8
My target goal of the week:

_____

I will address this goal by:

1._____

2._____

3._____

4._____

My progress towards this goal was:

How can I improve towards this goal area:

_____

_____

D. <u>Post Evaluation: Self Love Inventory</u>

1. I have the ability to make my own decisions.   1 2 3 4 5

2. I accept my imperfections.   1 2 3 4 5

3. When I'm alone, I enjoy myself.   1 2 3 4 5

4. I know I am a good person with a lot of qualities people love.

      1 2 3 4 5

5. It is easy for me to gain the acceptance of others. 1 2 3 4 5

6. I am pleased with who I am.   1 2 3 4 5

7. I do not allow people to disrespect or mistreat me.   1 2 3 4 5

8. I speak up when I feel I am being treated unfairly by others.

      1 2 3 4 5

9. I am pleased with where my life is headed.   1 2 3 4 5

Post Evaluation: Self Love Inventory cont...

10. When people criticize me, I listen to what they have to say, but I do not allow their comments to bring my self esteem down.

$$1 \; 2 \; 3 \; 4 \; 5$$

11. I believe I am unique and there is no one on earth like me.

$$1 \; 2 \; 3 \; 4 \; 5$$

12. I forgive myself for my past mistakes. $1 \; 2 \; 3 \; 4 \; 5$

13. I feel needed and loved by others. $1 \; 2 \; 3 \; 4 \; 5$

14. I have grown a lot from last year. $1 \; 2 \; 3 \; 4 \; 5$

15. I can imagine myself being more successful in a year or two.

$$1 \; 2 \; 3 \; 4 \; 5$$

E. Personal Notes

Love Thy Self - Teen Version

(For Ages 13-18

www.ingramcontent.com/pod-product-compliance
Lightning Source LLC
Chambersburg PA
CBHW081635040426

42449CB00014B/3330

TEXT OF THE 1919 VOLUME

The Panama Canal: The World's Greatest Engineering Feat

The Panama-Canal is a waterway connecting the Atlantic and Pacific Oceans, cut through the narrow neck of land connecting the continents of North and South America. On account of the great scale on which the work has been done, it has been quite impossible for the mind of the ordinary layman to grasp all its details. It will therefore not be inappropriate to give here a few statistics, which may help to bring home the magnitude of the work which has been performed.

Entering the Canal from the Atlantic Ocean in Limon Bay a ship proceeds up a sea level channel seven miles to Gatun, where it is lifted 85 feet by means of a flight of three locks, passing thence into Gatun Lake, an enormous artificially created sheet of water 164 square miles in area. This lake has been formed by impounding the waters of the Ohagres River by means of the great dam at Gatun. In the construction of this Dam, contrary to ordinary expectations, very little masonry has been used in proportion to its size. In appearance it is a huge mass of earth piled up across the valley joining the .hills on either side and forming part of the landscape. Its dimensions are: length 1½ miles, width at bottom ½ mile, at waterline 300 feet, and 100 feet at top, height 105 feet above sea level.

The Spillway is located about midway in the dam and is built through a natural hill, practically of solid rock, through which a channel 300 feet wide was cut. The Spillway is capable of discharging 154,000 cubic feet of water per second. The Hydroelectric Plant is. located on one side of the Spillway. This plant produces enough power to work the machinery of. the entire canal, run the Panama Rail Road and give light. for the whole Canal Zone.

After entering the lake a vessel may go at almost full speed for a distance of 23 miles, where it reaches the entrance to the Culebra Cut. The width of the channel through the lake varies from 1000 feet to 700 feet and through the cut narrows to 300 feet. Speed has to be reduced in passing through the Cut until Pedro Miguel. Lock has been reached.

At Pedro Miguel Lock the vessel is lowered 80 feet to the level of Miraflores Lake, a small artificial lake of about two square miles. Passing through Miraflores Lake the vessel arrives at Miraflores Locks, where it is lowered by two flights 55 feet to the sea level channel on the Pacific side whence it steams a distance of 8 miles to deep water in the Pacific.

The total length of the Canal from deep water to deep water is 50½ miles and the time occupied in passing through is from 10 to 12 hours according to the speed of the vessel. Three hours of this time are used in passing the locks.

The Culebra Cut, on which the most difficult portion of the work was encountered is nine miles long and has a bottom width of 800 feet, one-hundred and five million cubic yards of earth were taken from the cut, which goes right through the range of hills crossing the Isthmus.

At the Atlantic entrance to the canal is located the town of Colon, a vastly improved town to what Americans found it, when first beginning work on the canal. It has wide, straight and well laid out streets, is kept very clean and has a number of fine buildings. Here are located the fine Panama Canal Hospital and the Washington Hotel, a fine building of reinforced concrete in Spanish Mission . Style, capable of accommodating 175 guests and provided with every modern convenience.

Adjoining Colon is the American town of Cristobal with its fine Palm Avenue and dwellings for the employees of the Panama Canal. Here are also the offices of the Panama Rail Road Co., the new concrete piers fitted with the latest devices for quick loading and unloading of the largest vessels, as well as the Atlantic Terminal Coaling Plant, the largest of its kind in the world.

On the Pacific side is the City of Panama, the Capital of the Republic of the same name. It will be found a most interesting city with its Spanish style of architecture, fine old Cathedral and Churches, sea wall fortress and narrow and tortuous streets teeming with polyglot population.

Adjoining Panama is the American Settlement of Ancon, where the celebrated Ancon Hospital, the largest and finest tropical hospital of the world, the Tivoli Hotel, the largest and most popular hostelry on the Isthmus and numerous pretty flower clad cottages for the employees of the Panama Canal . are located. There are numerous pleasant and picturesque roads around Panama and Ancon, and 8 miles away are the ruins of the old City of Panama, which was destroyed and sacked by Morgan and his band of Pirates nearly two hundred and fifty years ago.

At the present time the Government of the, United States is contemplating' the construction of 500 miles of fine concrete roads in the Republic of Panama, leading to various points in the Interior. This will be welcome to tourists and visitors who for lack of good roads to the Interior have heretofore confined their visits to the two terminal cities and the canal, but who will soon be able to motor through some of the most beautiful tropical scenery and see the natives and study their customs in their homes. The Republic of Panama abounds in a beautiful Flora and Fauna as well as in a quantity of small and big game and the building of roads into the Interior of the country will give the sportsman opportunity to follow his inclination be it with the Rod and Reel, Scattergun or Rifle. The naturalist will find many specimens of insects and the botanist have opportunity to enlarge his collection of Ferns and Flowers as well as add some rare and valuable orchids to it.

SEAL OF THE CANAL ZONE ISTHMUS OF PANAMA

THE LAND DIVIDED THE WORLD UNITED

U.S.S. New Mexico

USS New Mexico (BB-40) was a battleship in service with the United States Navy from 1918 to 1946. She was the lead ship of a class of three battleships, and the first ship to be named for the state of New Mexico. Her keel was laid down on 14 October 1915 at the New York Navy Yard, she was launched on 20 May 1918. She was the first ship with a turbo-electric transmission, which helped her reach a cruising speed of 10 knots (19 km/h; 12 mph). Shortly after completing initial training, *New Mexico* escorted the ship that carried President Woodrow Wilson to Brest, France to sign the Treaty of Versailles. The interwar period was marked with repeated exercises with the Pacific and Atlantic Fleets, use as a trial ship for PID controllers, and a major modernization between March 1931 and January 1933.

The ship's first actions during World War II were neutrality patrols in the Atlantic Ocean. She returned to the Pacific after the Japanese attack on Pearl Harbor, and participated in shore bombardments during operations at Attu and Kiska, Tarawa, the Marshall Islands, the Mariana and Palau islands, Leyte, Luzon, and Okinawa. These were interspersed with escort duties, patrols, and refits. The ship was attacked by kamikazes on several occasions. *New Mexico* was present in Tokyo Bay for the signing of the Japanese Instrument of Surrender on 2 September 1945. Four days later, she sailed for the United States, and arrived in Boston on 17 October.

New Mexico was decommissioned in Boston on 19 July 1946, and struck from the Naval Vessel Register on 25 February 1947. The ship was sold for scrapping to the Lipsett Division of Luria Bros in November 1947, but attempts to bring the ship to Newark, New Jersey, for breaking up were met by resistance from city officials. City fireboats were sent to block the passage of the battleship and the Lipsett tugboats, while the United States Coast Guard declared intentions to guarantee safe passage. The Under Secretary of the Navy Department was sent to defuse what the media began to call the "Battle of Newark Bay," with the city agreeing to the breaking up of New Mexico and two other battleships before scrapping operations in Newark Bay ceased, and Lipsett under instructions to dismantle the ships in a set time frame or suffer financial penalties. Scrapping commenced in November and was completed by July 1948.

El New Mexico en las exclusas de Gatun, Canal de Panama.

U. S. S. New Mexico passing through Locks at Gatun, Panama Canal.

3

U.S. Submarine Chasers: SC-116

SC-116, the only identifiable vessel in this photo, was a submarine chaser in service with the United States Navy from 1917 to 1921. Her keel was laid down at Norfolk Navy Yard, Portsmouth, Virginia. She was commissioned on 14 November 1917. She displaced 99 tonnes, was 110' long, 13' 6" in the beam, and drafted 6' 3". Propelled by three 220hp Standard gasoline engines, her top speed was 17 knots and she carried a compliment of 26. Armament consisted of One 3"/23 gun mount, two .30 cal. machine guns, and one depth charge projector "Y Gun." After World War I, she was sold 24 June 1921 to Joseph G. Hitner of Philadelphia, Pennsylvania. Her ultimate disposition is unknown.

The SC-1 class was a large class of submarine chasers built during World War I for the United States Navy. They were ordered in very large numbers in order to combat attacks by German U-boats, with 442 boats built from 1917 to 1919. Deliveries started in July 1917, and continued into 1919, with 441 boats built, and the remaining seven boats canceled. One hundred were sold to France, and a further 121 US Navy SC boats were deployed to Europe to operate off Britain and France and in the Mediterranean, where they supported the Otranto Barrage with the remaining US Navy boats operating off the East Coast of the United States.

The US Navy lost six SC boats during World War I; USS SC-60 lost in collision with the tanker Fred M. Weller on 1 October 1918, USS SC-117 in a fire on 22 December 1917, USS SC-132 was lost in collision on 5 June 1918,[7] USS SC-187 in a collision on 4 August 1918, USS SC-209 by friendly fire from the trawler Felix Taussig on 27 August 1918, and USS SC-219 by fire on 19 February 1918.[8][10] France lost three SC-boats.

Following the end of the war, four boats (USS SC-274, USS SC-302, USS SC-311 and USS SC-312) were transferred to Cuba, while 14 boats were transferred to the United States Coast Guard in 1919–1920. Eight of the French SC boats remained in service at the outbreak of World War II. By December 1941, only 11 boats remained in US Navy service, with two continuing in use until at least April 1945. Two boats were sold to the Bulgarian Navy and saw action in World War II, sinking one Soviet submarine.

Caza Submarinos Americanos pasando el corte de Culebra, Canal de Panama.

U. S. Submarine Chasers passing Culebra Cut, Panama Canal.

U.S.S. Texas

USS Texas (BB-35), the second ship of the United States Navy named in honor of the U.S. state of Texas, is a New York-class battleship. The ship was launched on 18 May 1912 and commissioned on 12 March 1914.

Soon after her commissioning, *Texas* saw action in Mexican waters following the "Tampico Incident" and made numerous sorties into the North Sea during World War I. When the United States formally entered World War II in 1941, Texas escorted war convoys across the Atlantic and later shelled Axis-held beaches for the North African campaign and the Normandy Landings before being transferred to the Pacific Theater late in 1944 to provide naval gunfire support during the Battles of Iwo Jima and Okinawa. Texas was decommissioned in 1948, having earned a total of five battle stars for service in World War II, and is now a museum ship near Houston, Texas. In addition to her combat service, *Texas* also served as a technological testbed during her career, and in this capacity became the first US battleship to mount anti-aircraft guns, the first US ship to control gunfire with directors and range-keepers (analog forerunners of today's computers), the first US battleship to launch an aircraft, from a platform on Turret 2, and was one of the first to receive the CXAM-1 version of CXAM production radar in the US Navy.

Among the world's remaining battleships, *Texas* is notable for being the first modern steam powered, shaft driven US battleship, and the second battleship in the US navy to become a permanent museum ship, (the first being the USS Constitution commissioned as a permanent museum in 1907) and the first battleship declared to be a US National Historic Landmark., and is the only remaining World War I–era dreadnought battleship, though she is not the oldest surviving steel battleship: *Mikasa*, a pre-dreadnought battleship ordered in 1898 by the Imperial Japanese Navy is older than *Texas*. *Texas* is also noteworthy for being one of only seven remaining capital ship to have served in both World Wars.

El Texas en la recámara Central del Este exclusas de Gatun, Canal de Panama.

U. S. S. Texas in Middle East Chamber, Gatun Locks, Panama Canal.

7

U.S. Submarine Chasers SC-120 & 121

SC-120 was a submarine chaser in service with the United States Navy from 1917 to 1921. Her keel was laid down at Norfolk Navy Yard, Portsmouth, Virginia. She was commissioned on 4 October 1917. She displaced 99 tonnes, was 110' long, 13' 6" in the beam, and drafted 6' 3". Propelled by three 220hp Standard gasoline engines, her top speed was 17 knots and she carried a compliment of 26. Armament consisted of One 3"/23 gun mount, two .30 cal. machine guns, and one depth charge projector "Y Gun." After World War I, she was sold 20 July 1921 to Joseph G. Hitner of Philadelphia, Pennsylvania. Her ultimate disposition is unknown.

SC-121 was a submarine chaser in service with the United States Navy from 1917 to 1921. Her keel was laid down at Norfolk Navy Yard, Portsmouth, Virginia. She was commissioned on 16 October 1917. She displaced 99 tonnes, was 110' long, 13' 6" in the beam, and drafted 6' 3". Propelled by three 220hp Standard gasoline engines, her top speed was 17 knots and she carried a compliment of 26. Armament consisted of One 3"/23 gun mount, two .30 cal. machine guns, and one depth charge projector "Y Gun." After World War I, she was sold 24 June 1921 to Joseph G. Hitner of Philadelphia, Pennsylvania. Her ultimate disposition is unknown.

Seis Caza Submarinos Americanos en las exclusas de Gatun, Canal de Panama.

U. S. Submarine Chasers being locked at Gatun, Panama Canal.

Gatun Dam Spillway

The Gatun Dam is a large earthen dam across the Chagres River in Panama, near the town of Gatun. The dam, constructed between 1907 and 1913, is a crucial element of the Panama Canal; it impounds the artificial Gatun Lake, which in turn carries ships for 33 kilometers (21 mi) of their transit across the Isthmus of Panama. In addition, a hydro-electric generating station at the dam generates electricity which is used to operate the locks and other equipment in the canal.

The spillway for the dam is constructed on the central hill; it consists of a semi-circular concrete dam, which regulates the flow of water down a concrete channel built into the back slope of the hill. The spillway dam itself measures 225 meters (738 ft) along the top; its crest is at 16 feet (4.9 m) below the normal lake level. The spillway is designed so that water pouring over the semi-circular dam converges at the bottom from opposite directions and neutralizes its own force, thus minimizing erosion below.

The spillway dam is topped by 14 gates, supported by concrete piers and each 14 meters (46 ft) wide by 6 meters (20 ft) high. These gates, which are electrically operated, are raised or lowered to control the flow of water; with the lake level at 26.5 meters (87 ft), its planned maximum level, the capacity of the spillway is 4,100 cubic meters (140,000 cu ft) per second, more than the maximum flow of the Chagres River. In addition to this, the culverts in the locks can dispose of 1,400 cubic meters (49,000 cu ft) per second.

Construction of the dam was a great engineering achievement, eclipsed only by the parallel excavation of the Culebra Cut; at the time of completion, the dam was the largest earth dam in the world, and Lake Gatun was the largest artificial lake in the world.

10

Desague de Gatun funcionando, Canal de Panama.

Gatun Spillway in Operation, Panama Canal.

11

U.S.S. Rhode Island

USS Rhode Island (BB-17) was the last of five Virginia-class battleships built for the United States Navy, and was the second ship to carry her name. She was laid down in May 1902, launched in May 1904, and commissioned into the Atlantic Fleet in February 1906. The ship was armed with an offensive battery of four 12-inch (305 mm) guns and eight 8-inch (203 mm) guns, and she was capable of a top speed of 19 knots (35 km/h; 22 mph).

The ship was armed with a main battery of four 12-inch/40 caliber Mark 4[a] guns in two twin gun turrets on the centerline, one forward and aft. The secondary battery consisted of eight 8-inch/45 caliber guns and twelve 6-inch (152 mm)/50 caliber guns. The 8-inch guns were mounted in four twin turrets; two of these were superposed atop the main battery turrets, with the other two turrets abreast the forward funnel. The 6-inch guns were placed in casemates in the hull. For close-range defense against torpedo boats, she carried twelve 3-inch (76 mm)/50 caliber guns mounted in casemates along the side of the hull and twelve 3-pounder guns. She also carried two 1-pounder guns. As was standard for capital ships of the period, Rhode Island carried four 21 inch (533 mm) torpedo tubes, submerged in her hull on the broadside.

The ship's career primarily consisted of training with the other battleships of the Atlantic Fleet. *Rhode Island* took part in the cruise of the Great White Fleet in 1907–1909, and thereafter largely remained in the Atlantic. In late 1913, she cruised the Caribbean coast of Mexico to protect American interests during the Mexican Revolution. After the United States entered World War I in April 1917, *Rhode Island* was assigned to anti-submarine patrols off the east coast of the US. Starting in December 1918, after the end of the war, the ship was used to repatriate American soldiers. She carried over 5,000 men in the course of five trips. She was briefly transferred to the Pacific Fleet in 1919 before being decommissioned in 1920 and sold for scrap in 1923 under the terms of the Washington Naval Treaty.

Rhode Island was 441 feet 3 inches (134.49 m) long overall and had a beam of 76 ft 3 in (23.24 m) and a draft of 23 ft 9 in (7.24 m). She displaced 14,948 long tons (15,188 t) as designed and up to 16,094 long tons (16,352 t) at full load. The ship was powered by two-shaft triple-expansion steam engines rated at 19,000 indicated horsepower (14,000 kW) and twelve coal-fired Babcock & Wilcox boilers, generating a top speed of 19 knots (35 km/h; 22 mph). As built, she was fitted with heavy military masts, but these were quickly replaced by cage masts in 1909. She had a crew of 812 officers and enlisted men.

El Rhode Island en el lago Gatun, Canal de Panama.

U. S. S. Rhode Island in Gatun Lake, Panama Canal.

U.S.S. North Carolina

USS North Carolina (ACR-12/CA-12) was a Tennessee-class armored cruiser of the United States Navy. The ship was built by Newport News Shipbuilding; she was laid down in March 1905, launched in October 1906, and was commissioned in May 1908. The final class of armored cruisers to be built for the US Navy, *North Carolina* and her sisters were armed with a main battery of four 10-inch (254 mm) guns, and were capable of a top speed of 22 knots (41 km/h; 25 mph).

North Carolina was armed with a main battery of four 10-inch (254 mm) 40-caliber Mark 3 guns in two twin gun turrets, one forward and one aft. These were supported by a secondary battery of sixteen 6-inch (152 mm) 40-caliber Mark 8 guns mounted in casemates, eight on each broadside. For defense against torpedo boats, she carried twenty-two 3-inch (76 mm) 50-caliber guns in single pedestal mounts either in casemates or sponsons in the hull. She also carried a variety of smaller guns, including twelve 3-pounder automatic guns and four 1-pounders. Like other contemporary armored cruisers, she was also armed with four 21 inches (533 mm) torpedo tubes located below the waterline in her hull.

North Carolina spent much of her career in the Atlantic Ocean and Caribbean Sea conducting training and visiting foreign countries. She went on short deployments to the Mediterranean Sea twice, the first in 1909 to protect American citizens in the Ottoman Empire, and the second during World War I, again to protect still neutral American citizens in the region. After the United States entered the war in April 1917, *North Carolina* was used to escort troop ships off the eastern coast of the United States. Following the war in late 1918 and early 1919, she was used to carry soldiers from the American Expeditionary Force back from France. In 1920, the ship was renamed *Charlotte* so her original name could be used for a new battleship, and she was decommissioned the following year. She was sold for scrap in September 1930 and broken up thereafter.

14

El North Carolina entrando el corte de Culebra, Canal de Panama.

U. S. S. North Carolina entering the Culebra Cut, Panama Canal.

15

U.S.S. Vermont

USS Vermont (BB-20), a Connecticut-class battleship, was the second ship of the United States Navy named after the 14th state. She was the third member of the class, which included five other ships. The Connecticut-class ships were armed with a main battery of four 12-inch (300 mm) guns and had a top speed of 19 knots (35 km/h; 22 mph). Vermont was laid down in May 1904 at the Fore River shipyard and launched in August 1905. The ship entered service with the Atlantic Fleet in March 1907.

The ship was armed with a main battery of four 12 inch /45 Mark 5 guns in two twin gun turrets on the centerline, one forward and aft. The secondary battery consisted of eight 8-inch (203 mm) /45 guns and twelve 7-inch (178 mm) /45 guns. The 8-inch guns were mounted in four twin turrets amidships and the 7-inch guns were placed in casemates along the side of the hull. For close-range defense against torpedo boats, she carried twenty 3-inch (76 mm) /50 guns mounted in casemates along the side of the hull and twelve 3-pounder guns. She also carried four 37 mm (1.5 in) 1-pounder guns. As was standard for capital ships of the period, Vermont carried four 21 inch (533 mm) torpedo tubes, submerged in her hull on the broadside.

Shortly after she entered service, *Vermont* joined the Great White Fleet for its circumnavigation of the globe in 1908–1909. She took part in the international Hudson–Fulton Celebration in New York in 1909 and made trips to Europe in 1910 and 1913. Thereafter, the ship became involved in interventions in several Central American countries, including the United States occupation of Veracruz during the Mexican Revolution, where two of her crew earned the Medal of Honor. During the United States' participation in World War I from April 1917 to November 1918, Vermont served as a training ship for engine room personnel. From November 1918 to June 1919, she made a series of trips to return American soldiers from Europe before being decommissioned in June 1920. She was sold for scrap in November 1923 according to the terms of the Washington Naval Treaty. Her bell currently resides at the Vermont State Capitol in Montpelier, Vermont.

16

El *Vermont* pasando las exclusas de Gatun, Canal de Panama.

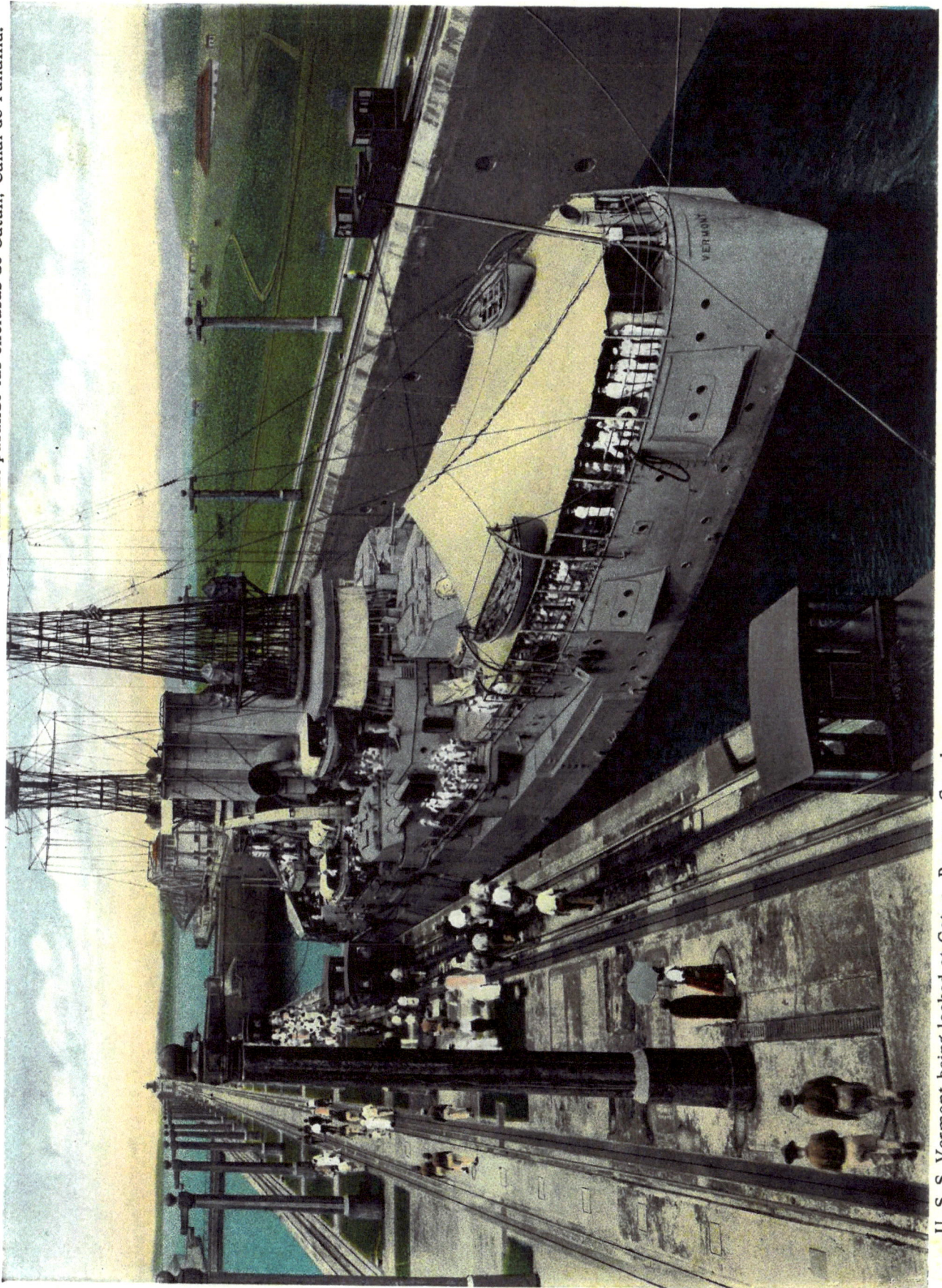

U. S. S. Vermont being locked at Gatun, Panama Canal.

17

U.S.S. Rhode Island

USS Rhode Island was laid down at the Fore River Shipyard in Massachusetts on 1 May 1902 and was launched on 17 May 1904,[2] to little fanfare due to a worker strike at the shipyard. Upon launching, the ship became stuck on a mud bank where she remained before being towed afloat two days later. The ship was completed a year later, and on 19 February 1906 commissioned into the fleet. The ship conducted an extensive shakedown cruise and sea trials before steaming to Hampton Roads, where she was assigned to the 2nd Division of the 1st Squadron, Atlantic Fleet on 1 January 1907. She left Hampton Roads on 9 March 1907, bound for Guantanamo Bay, Cuba. There, she and the rest of the 1st Squadron conducted maneuvers and gunnery training. After the conclusion of these exercises, she returned to the east coast of the United States for a cruise to Cape Cod Bay.

On 8 December, *Rhode Island* returned to Hampton Roads, where she and fifteen other battleships held a naval review at the start of the cruise of the Great White Fleet. The battleships were joined by transports and a squadron of torpedo boats. On 16 December, President Theodore Roosevelt reviewed the fleet before it departed on the first leg of the trip. The cruise of the Great White Fleet was conceived as a way to demonstrate American military power, particularly to Japan. Tensions had begun to rise between the United States and Japan after the latter's victory in the Russo-Japanese War in 1905, particularly over racist opposition to Japanese immigration to the United States. The press in both countries began to call for war, and Roosevelt hoped to use the demonstration of naval might to deter Japanese aggression. The fleet cruised south to the Caribbean and then to South America, making stops in Port of Spain, Rio de Janeiro, Punta Arenas, and Valparaíso, among other cities. After arriving in Mexico in March 1908, the fleet spent three weeks conducting gunnery practice.

The fleet then resumed its voyage up the Pacific coast of the Americas, stopping in San Francisco and Seattle before crossing the Pacific to Australia, stopping in Hawaii on the way. Stops in the South Pacific included Melbourne, Sydney, and Auckland. The fleet then turned north for the Philippines, stopping in Manila, before continuing on to Japan where a welcoming ceremony was held in Yokohama. Three weeks of exercises followed in Subic Bay in the Philippines in November. The ships passed Singapore on 6 December and entered the Indian Ocean; they coaled in Colombo before proceeding to the Suez Canal and coaling again at Port Said, Egypt. The fleet called in several Mediterranean ports before stopping in Gibraltar, where an international fleet of British, Russian, French, and Dutch warships greeted the Americans. The ships then crossed the Atlantic to return to Hampton Roads on 22 February 1909, having traveled 46,729 nautical miles (86,542 km; 53,775 mi). There, they conducted a naval review for Theodore Roosevelt. (*See also page 12-13.*)

18

El Rhode Island entrando el corte de Culebra. Canal de Panama.

U. S. S. Rhode Island passing Culebra Cut, Panama Canal.

19

U.S.S. Mississippi

USS Mississippi (BB-41/AG-128), the second of three members of the New Mexico class of battleship, was the third ship of the United States Navy named in honor of the 20th state. The ship was built at the Newport News Shipbuilding Company of Newport News, Virginia, from her keel laying in April 1915, her launching in January 1917, and her commissioning in December that year. She was armed with a battery of twelve 14-inch (356 mm) guns in four three-gun turrets, and was protected by heavy armor plate, with her main belt armor being 13.5 inches (343 mm) thick.

The ship was armed with a main battery of twelve 14-inch (356 mm)/50 caliber guns in four, three-gun turrets on the centerline, placed in two superfiring pairs forward and aft of the superstructure. Unlike earlier American battleships with triple turrets, these mounts were true three-gun barrels, in that each barrel could elevate independently. The secondary battery consisted of fourteen 5-inch (127 mm)/51 caliber guns mounted in individual casemates clustered in the superstructure amidships. Initially, the ship was to have been fitted with twenty-two of the guns, but experiences in the North Sea during World War I demonstrated that the additional guns, which would have been placed in the hull, would have been unusable in anything but calm seas. As a result, the casemates were plated over to prevent flooding. The secondary battery was augmented with four 3-inch (76 mm)/50 caliber guns. In addition to her gun armament, Mississippi was also fitted with two 21-inch (530 mm) torpedo tubes, mounted submerged in the hull, one on each broadside.

The ship remained in North American waters during World War I, conducting training exercises to work up the crew. Throughout the 1920s and 1930s, the ship served in the Pacific Fleet. In May 1941, with World War II and the Battle of the Atlantic raging, Mississippi and her two sister ships were transferred to the Atlantic Fleet to help protect American shipping through the Neutrality Patrols. Two days after the Japanese attack on Pearl Harbor, *Mississippi* departed the Atlantic to return to the Pacific Fleet; throughout her participation in World War II, she supported amphibious operations in the Pacific. She shelled Japanese forces during the Gilbert and Marshall Islands and the Philippines campaigns and the invasions of Peleliu and Okinawa. The Japanese fleet attacked American forces during the Philippines campaign, and in the ensuing Battle of Leyte Gulf, Mississippi took part in the Battle of Surigao Strait, the last battleship engagement in history.

After the war, *Mississippi* was converted into a gunnery training ship, and was also used to test new weapons systems. These included the RIM-2 Terrier missile and the AUM-N-2 Petrel missile. She was eventually decommissioned in 1956 and sold to ship breakers in November that year.

El Mississippi en las exclusas de Pedro Miguel, Canal de Panama.

U. S. S. Mississippi being locked at Pedro Miguel, Panama Canal.

U.S.S. Vermont

The keel for *Vermont* was laid down on 21 May 1904 at the Fore River Shipyard in Quincy, Massachusetts. The completed hull was launched on 31 August 1905, with the christening performed by Jennie Bell, the daughter of Charles J. Bell, the governor of the ship's namesake state. On 4 March 1907, *Vermont* was commissioned into the US Navy at the Boston Navy Yard, with Captain William P. Potter as her first commanding officer. The ship then embarked on a shakedown cruise from Boston to Hampton Roads, Virginia. She then joined the 1st Division of the Atlantic Fleet for training exercises. *Vermont* left Hampton Roads on 30 August, bound for Provincetown. She stayed there until 5 September before returning to the Boston Navy Yard two days later for repairs that lasted until November. On 30 November, the ship left Boston to begin preparations to join the world cruise of the Great White Fleet.

Her first two stops were in Rhode Island; she took on coal in Bradford before moving to Newport, where she loaded stores. She then steamed to Tompkinsville, New York to receive her full stock of ammunition. The ship arrived in Hampton Roads on 8 December, where she joined the rest of the Great White Fleet, which was commanded by Rear Admiral Robley D. Evans. *Vermont* and fifteen other battleships began their voyage on 16 December. The fleet cruised south to the Caribbean and then to South America, making stops in Port of Spain, Rio de Janeiro, Punta Arenas, and Valparaíso, among other cities. After arriving in Mexico in March 1908, the fleet spent three weeks conducting gunnery practice. The fleet then resumed its voyage up the Pacific coast of the Americas, stopping in San Francisco and Seattle before crossing the Pacific to Australia, stopping in Hawaii on the way. Stops in the South Pacific included Melbourne, Sydney, and Auckland.

After leaving Australia, the fleet turned north for the Philippines, stopping in Manila, before continuing on to Japan where a welcoming ceremony was held in Yokohama. Three weeks of exercises followed in Subic Bay in the Philippines in November. The ships passed Singapore on 6 December and entered the Indian Ocean; they coaled in Colombo before proceeding to the Suez Canal and coaling again at Port Said, Egypt. The fleet called in several Mediterranean ports before stopping in Gibraltar, where an international fleet of British, Russian, French, and Dutch warships greeted the Americans. The ships then crossed the Atlantic to return to Hampton Roads on 22 February 1909, having traveled 46,729 nautical miles (86,542 km; 53,775 mi). There, they conducted a naval review for President Theodore Roosevelt. During the cruise, Captain Potter was promoted to Rear Admiral and advanced to the 1st Division commander; his place as *Vermont's* commander was taken by Captain Frank Friday Fletcher. (*See also pages 16-17.*)

22

El Vermont saliendo de la recamara superior Oeste, exclusas de Gatun, Canal de Panama.

U. S. S. Vermont leaving Upper West Chamber, Gatun Locks, Panama Canal.

U.S.S. Wyoming

USS Wyoming (BB-32) was the lead ship of her class of dreadnought battleships and was the third ship of the United States Navy named Wyoming, although she was only the second named in honor of the 44th state. *Wyoming* was laid down at the William Cramp & Sons in Philadelphia in February 1910, was launched in May 1911, and was completed in September 1912. She was armed with a main battery of twelve 12-inch (305 mm) guns and capable of a top speed of 20.5 kn (38.0 km/h; 23.6 mph).

The ship was armed with a main battery of twelve 12-inch/50 caliber Mark 7 guns in six Mark 9 twin gun turrets on the centerline, two of which were placed in a superfiring pair forward. The other four turrets were placed aft of the superstructure in two superfiring pairs. The secondary battery consisted of twenty-one 5-inch (127 mm)/51 caliber guns mounted in casemates along the side of the hull.

During the First World War, she was part of the Battleship Division Nine, which was attached to the British Grand Fleet as the 6th Battle Squadron. During the war, she was primarily tasked with patrolling in the North Sea and escorting convoys to Norway. She served in both the Atlantic and Pacific Fleets throughout the 1920s, and in 1931–1932, she was converted into a training ship according to the terms of the London Naval Treaty of 1930.

Wyoming served as a training ship throughout the 1930s, and in November 1941, she became a gunnery ship. She operated primarily in the Chesapeake Bay area, which earned her the nickname "Chesapeake Raider". In this capacity, she trained some 35,000 gunners for the hugely expanded US Navy during World War II. She continued in this duty until 1947, when she was decommissioned on 1 August and subsequently sold for scrap; she was broken up in New York starting in December 1947.

24

El Wyoming en las exclusas de Pedro Miguel, Canal de Panama.

U. S. S. Wyoming in Pedro Miguel Locks, Panama Canal.

U.S.S. New York

USS New York (BB-34) was a United States Navy battleship, the lead ship of her class. Named for New York State, she was designed as the first ship to carry the 14-inch (356 mm)/45-caliber gun.

Her armament consisted of ten 14-inch/45-caliber guns which could be elevated to 15 degrees, and arrayed in five double mounts designated, from bow to stern, 1, 2, 3, 4, and 5. The class was the last to feature a turret mounted amidships. As built, she also carried twenty-one 5-inch (127 mm)/51-caliber guns, primarily for defense against destroyers and torpedo boats. The 5-inch guns were poor in accuracy in rough seas due to the open casemates mounted in the hull, so the 5-inch armament was reduced to 16 guns in 1918 by removal of the least useful positions near the ends of the ship. The ship was not designed with anti-aircraft (AA) defense in mind, but two 3-inch (76 mm)/50 caliber AA guns were added in 1918. She also had four 21-inch (533 mm) torpedo tubes, 1 each on the port side bow and stern and starboard bow and stern, for the Bliss-Leavitt Mark 3 torpedo. The torpedo rooms held 12 torpedoes total, plus 12 naval defense mines. Her crew consisted of 1,042 officers and enlisted men.

Entering service in 1914, she was part of the U.S. Navy force which was sent to reinforce the British Grand Fleet in the North Sea near the end of World War I. During that time, she was involved in at least two incidents with German U-boats, and is believed to have been the only US ship to have sunk one in the war, during an accidental collision in October 1918. Following the war, she was sent on a litany of training exercises and cruises in both the Atlantic and the Pacific, and saw several overhauls to increase her armament, aircraft handling and armor.

She entered the Neutrality Patrol at the beginning of World War II, and served as a convoy escort for ships to Iceland and Great Britain in the early phase of the war. She saw her first combat against coastal artillery during Operation Torch around Casablanca in North Africa, and later became a training ship. Late in the war, she moved to the Pacific, and provided naval gunfire support for the invasion of Iwo Jima and later the invasion of Okinawa. Returning to Pearl Harbor for repairs until the end of the war, she was classified obsolete and was chosen to take part in the Operation Crossroads nuclear weapon tests at Bikini Atoll in 1946. She survived both explosions and the effects of radiation on the ship were studied for several years. She was eventually sunk as a target in 1948. She received three battle stars for her service

El New York en las exclusas de Pedro Miguel, Canal de Panama.

U. S. S. New York in East Chamber, Pedro Miguel Locks, Panama Canal.

The Great White Fleet

The Great White Fleet was the popular nickname for the powerful United States Navy battleships which completed a journey around the globe from 16 December 1907, to 22 February 1909, by order of United States President Theodore Roosevelt. Its mission was to make friendly courtesy visits to numerous countries, while displaying new U.S. naval power to the world.

It consisted of 16 battleships divided into two squadrons, along with various escorts. Roosevelt sought to demonstrate growing American military power and blue-water navy capability. Hoping to enforce treaties and protect overseas holdings, the United States Congress appropriated funds to build American naval power. Beginning in the 1880s with just 90 small ships, over one-third of them wooden and therefore obsolete, the navy quickly grew to include new steel fighting vessels. The hulls of these ships were painted a stark white, giving the armada the nickname "Great White Fleet."

Background and purpose

In the twilight of his administration, United States President Theodore Roosevelt dispatched sixteen U.S. Navy battleships of the Atlantic Fleet on a worldwide voyage of circumnavigation from 16 December 1907 to 22 February 1909. The hulls were painted white, the Navy's peacetime color scheme, decorated with gilded scrollwork with a red, white, and blue banner on their bows. These ships would later come to be known as the Great White Fleet.

The purpose of the fleet deployment was multifaceted. Ostensibly, it served as a showpiece of American goodwill, as the fleet visited numerous countries and harbors. In this, the voyage was not unprecedented. Naval courtesy calls, many times in conjunction with the birthdays of various monarchs and other foreign celebrations, had become common in the 19th century. Port calls showcased pomp, ceremony, and militarism during a period of rising pre-war nationalism. In 1891, a large French fleet visited Kronstadt, Russia, in conjunction with negotiations between the two nations. Although France and Russia had been hostile to each other for at least three decades prior, the significance of the call was not lost on Russia, and Tsar Nicholas II signed a treaty of alliance with France in 1894. As navies grew larger, naval pageants grew longer, more elaborate, and more frequent. The United States began participating in these events in 1902 when Roosevelt invited Kaiser Wilhelm II of Germany to send a squadron for a courtesy call to New York City. Invitations for U.S. Navy ships to participate in fleet celebrations in the United Kingdom, France, and Germany followed.

Additionally, the voyage of the Great White Fleet demonstrated both at home and on the world stage that the U.S. had become a major sea power in the years after its triumph in the Spanish–American War, with possessions that included Guam, the Philippines, and Puerto Rico. This was not the first demonstration of naval power however; during the Algeciras Conference in 1906, which was convened to settle a diplomatic crisis between France and Germany over the fate of Morocco, Roosevelt had ordered eight battleships to maintain a presence in the Mediterranean Sea. Since Japan had arisen as a major sea power with the 1905 annihilation of the Russian fleet at Tsushima, the deployment of the Great White Fleet was therefore intended, at least in part, to send a message to Tokyo that the American fleet could be deployed anywhere, even from its Atlantic ports, and would be able to defend American interests in the Philippines and the Pacific.

That gesture capitalized on diplomatic trouble that had resulted from anti-Japanese riots in San Francisco. Those problems had been resolved by the Gentlemen's Agreement of 1907 and the fleet visit was a friendly gesture to Japan. The Japanese welcomed it. Roosevelt saw the deployment as one that would encourage patriotism, and give the impression that he would teach Japan "a lesson in polite behavior", as historian Robert A. Hart phrased

Balboa Coaling Plant with Dry Docks in Background, Panama Canal.

it. After the fleet had crossed the Pacific, Japanese statesmen realized that the balance of power in the East had changed since the Root–Takahira Agreement that defined relevant spheres of interest of the United States and Japan.

The voyage also provided an opportunity to improve the sea- and battle-worthiness of the fleet. While earlier capital ship classes such as the *Kearsarge*, *Illinois* and *Maine* were designed primarily for coastal defense, later classes such as the *Virginia* and *Connecticut* incorporated lessons learned from the Spanish–American War and were conceived as ships with "the highest practicable speed and the greatest radius of action", in the words of the appropriation bills approved by the United States Congress for their construction. They were intended as modern warships capable of long-range operations. Nevertheless, the experience gained in the recent war

with Spain had been limited.

Concerns and preparations

Roosevelt's stated intent was to give the navy practice in navigation, communication, coal consumption and fleet maneuvering; navy professionals maintained, however, that such matters could be served better in home waters. In light of what had happened to the Russian Baltic Fleet, they were concerned about sending their own fleet on a long deployment, especially since part of the intent was to impress a modern, battle-tested navy that had not known defeat. The fleet was untested in making such a voyage, and Tsushima had proven that extended deployments had no place in practical strategy. The Japanese Navy was close to coaling and repair facilities; while American ships could coal in the Philippines, docking facilities were far from optimal. An extended stop on the West

29

Coast of the United States during the voyage for overhaul and refurbishment in dry dock would be a necessity. Planning for the voyage, however, showed a dearth of adequate facilities there, as well. The main sea channel of the Mare Island Navy Yard near San Francisco was too shallow for battleships, which left only the Puget Sound Navy Yard in Bremerton, Washington, for refit and repair. The Hunter's Point civilian yard in San Francisco could accommodate capital ships, but had been closed due to lack of use and was slated for demolition. President Roosevelt ordered that Hunter's Point be reopened, facilities be brought up to date, and the fleet to report there.

Also, the question of adequate resources for coaling existed. This was not an issue when the Atlantic Fleet cruised the Atlantic or Caribbean, as fuel supplies were readily available. However, the United States did not enjoy a worldwide network of coaling stations like that of Great Britain, nor did it have an adequate supply of auxiliary vessels for resupply. During the Spanish–American War, this lack had forced Admiral George Dewey to buy a collier-load of British coal in Hong Kong before the Battle of Manila Bay to ensure his squadron would not run out of steam at sea. The need had been even more pressing for the Russian Baltic Fleet during its long deployment during the Russo-Japanese War, not just for the distance it was to steam, but also because, as a belligerent nation in wartime, most neutral ports were closed to it due to international law. While the lack of support vessels was pointed out and a vigorous program of building such ships suggested by Rear Admiral George W. Melville, who had served as chief of the Bureau of Equipment, his words were not heeded adequately until World War II.

Federal regulations that restricted supply vessels for Navy ships to those flying the United States flag, complicated by the lack of an adequate United States Merchant Marine, proved another obstacle. Roosevelt initially offered to award Navy supply contracts to American skippers whose bids exceeded those of foreign captains by less than 50 percent. Many carriers declined this offer because they could not obtain enough cargo to cover the cost of the return trip. Two months before the fleet sailed, Roosevelt ordered the Navy Department to contract 38 ships to supply the fleet with the 125,000 tons of coal it would need to steam from Hampton Roads, Virginia, to San Francisco. Only eight of these were American-registered; most of the other 30 were of British registry. This development was potentially awkward, since part of the mission was to impress Japan with the perception of overwhelming American naval power. Britain had become a military ally of Japan in 1905 with the Anglo-Japanese Alliance, which obliged it to aid Japan should a foreign power declare war against it. Technically, the list of potential combatants included the United States. The British government decided to play both sides of the political fence with the intent of moderating any Japanese-American friction that might arise.

Voyage

As the Panama Canal was not yet complete, the fleet had to pass through the Straits of Magellan. The scope of such an operation was unprecedented in U.S. history, as ships had to sail from all points of the compass to rendezvous points and proceed according to a carefully orchestrated, well-conceived plan. It involved almost the entire operational capability of the U.S. Navy. Unlike the formidable obstacles that had faced the Russian fleet on its voyage from the Baltic to the Pacific, which eventually led to its destruction by the Japanese in 1905, the U.S. effort benefitted from a peaceful environment which aided the coordination of ship movements.

In port after port, citizens in the thousands turned out to see and greet the fleet. In 1908, the Great White Fleet visited Monterey, California, from 1–4 May. The nearby Hotel Del Monte in Del Monte, California, hosted a grand ball for the officers of the fleet.

In Australia, the arrival of the Great White Fleet on 20 August 1908 was used to encourage support for the forming of Australia's own navy. In Sicily, the sailors helped in recovery operations after the 1908 Messina earthquake.

Palm Avenue, Hospital Grounds, Ancon, Canal Zone.

Vista trasera del Edificio de Administracion del Canal de Panama, Balboa, Zona del Canal.

Panama Canal Administration Building, Rear View, Balboa, Canal Zone.

31

Fleet composition

The fourteen-month-long voyage was a grand pageant of American naval power. The squadrons were manned by 14,000 sailors. They covered some 43,000 nautical miles (80,000 km) and made twenty port calls on six continents. The fleet was impressive, especially as a demonstration of American industrial prowess (all eighteen ships had been constructed since the Spanish–American War), but already the battleships represented the suddenly outdated 'pre-dreadnought' type of capital ship, as the first battleships of the revolutionary Dreadnought class had just entered service, and the U.S. Navy's first dreadnought, *South Carolina*, was already fitting out. The two oldest ships in the fleet, *Kearsarge* and *Kentucky*, were already obsolete and unfit for battle; two others, *Maine* and *Alabama*, had to be detached at San Francisco because of mechanical troubles and were replaced by the *Nebraska* and the *Wisconsin*. (After repairs, *Alabama* and *Maine* completed their "own, more direct, circumnavigation of the globe" via Honolulu, Guam, Manila, Singapore, Colombo, Suez, Naples, Gibraltar, the Azores, and finally back to the United States, arriving on 20 October 1908, four months before the remainder of the fleet, which had taken a more circuitous route.)

The battleships were accompanied during the first leg of their voyage by a "Torpedo Flotilla" of six early destroyers, as well as by several auxiliary ships. The destroyers and their tender did not actually steam in company with the battleships, but followed their own itinerary from Hampton Roads, Virginia to San Francisco, California. Also of note is that the armored cruiser *Washington* preceded the Fleet itinerary for its first and second legs by about a month, perhaps making arrangements to later receive the Fleet.

General fleet itinerary

With *Connecticut* as flagship under the command of Rear Admiral Robley D. Evans, the fleet sailed from Hampton Roads on 16 December 1907 for Trinidad, British West Indies, thence to Rio de Janeiro, Brazil; Punta Arenas, Chile; Callao, Peru; Magdalena Bay, Mexico, and up the West Coast, arriving at San Francisco, 6 May 1908.

At San Francisco, Rear Admiral Charles S. Sperry assumed command of the fleet, owing to the poor health of Admiral Evans. Also at San Francisco, the squadrons were slightly rearranged, bringing the newest and best ships in the fleet up to the First Squadron. *Glacier* was detached and later became the supply ship of the Pacific Fleet. At this time also, *Nebraska*, under Captain Reginald F. Nicholson, and *Wisconsin*, under Captain Frank E. Beatty, were substituted for *Maine* and *Alabama*. In San Francisco, *Minnesota* was brought forward into First Squadron, First Division, and *Louisiana* took her place as flagship, Second Squadron.

Leaving that port on 7 July 1908 the U.S. Atlantic Fleet visited Honolulu; Auckland, New Zealand; Sydney, Melbourne, and Albany, Australia; Manila, Philippines; Yokohama, Japan; and Colombo, Ceylon; then arriving at Suez, Egypt, on 3 January 1909.

While the fleet was in Egypt, word was received of an earthquake in Sicily, thus affording an opportunity for the United States to show its friendship to Italy by offering aid to the sufferers. *Connecticut, Illinois, Culgoa*, and *Yankton* were dispatched to Messina, Italy, at once. The crew of *Illinois* recovered the bodies of the American consul, Arthur S. Cheney, and his wife, entombed in the ruins.

Scorpion, the fleet's station ship at Constantinople, and *Celtic*, a refrigerator ship fitted out in New York, were hurried to Messina, relieving *Connecticut* and *Illinois*, so that they could continue on the cruise.

Leaving Messina on 9 January 1909, the fleet stopped at Naples, Italy, thence to Gibraltar, arriving at Hampton Roads on 22 February 1909. There, President Roosevelt reviewed the fleet as it passed into the roadstead.

Experience gained

The cruise of the Great White Fleet provided practical experience for US naval personnel in sea duty and ship handling. It also showed the viability of US warships for long-range operations as no major

Iglesia y Plaza de la Catedral, Panama, Republica de Pamama.

Cathedral Church and Plaza, Panama, Republic of Panama

Plaza de la Catedral y Calle 5a, mostrando el Hotel Central, Panama, Republica de Panama.

Cathedral Plaza and 5th Street, showing Hotel Central, Panama.

33

mechanical mishaps occurred. However, while the cruise uncovered design flaws, it did not test the abilities to engage in battle fleet action. In fact, the success of the deployment might have helped obscure design deficiencies that were not addressed until World War I. These included excessive draft, low armor belts, large turret openings and exposed ammunition hoists.

Effects on US capital ship design

While the capital ships of the Great White Fleet were already obsolescent in light of the "big gun" revolution ushered in by the construction of HMS Dreadnought, their behavior at sea furnished valuable information that affected future construction. For instance, in terms of seaworthiness, all the capital ships in the fleet proved wet in all but the calmest seas, which led to the flared bows of subsequent U.S. battleships, increased freeboard forward and such spray-reducing measures as the elimination of billboards for anchors and gun sponsons. Increased freeboard was needed; this and related considerations demanded increases in beam and overall size. Between the Florida-class battleships, the last American capital ships completed before data from the cruise became available, and the Wyoming class, the first designed after this data was received, displacement (and, as a result, cost) per ship increased by one third.

Deficiencies in seaworthiness in turn reduced the battle-worthiness of the fleet. Turret heights for main armament proved too low and needed to be raised. Secondary armament was useless at speed and especially in tradewind conditions (with the wind moving over the sea at 10 knots (19 km/h) or greater) and needed to be moved much higher in the hull. Improved placement began with the Wyoming-class battleships and was further refined in the Nevada class. Casemates for the bow 3-inch guns in the newer pre-dreadnoughts were untenable due to wetness and were removed. Another discovery was that, even when fully loaded, the bottom of the battleships' side armor was visible—and the ships thus vulnerable to shells that might hit beneath it to reach their machinery and magazines—in smooth to moderate seas. The profile of crests and troughs in some ships contributed to this problem. Admiral

Evans concluded that the standard 8-foot (2.4 m) width of belt armor was inadequate.

One other necessity the cruise outlined was the need for tactical homogeneity. Before the cruise, critics such as then-Captain William Sims (to whom President Roosevelt listened) had argued that American warship design had remained too conservative and precluded the level of efficiency needed for the fleet to function as an effective unit. The cruise proved the charge true. This would eventually lead to the building of standard type battleships in the U.S. Navy. When President Roosevelt convened the 1908 Newport Conference of the Naval War College, he placed responsibility for U.S. battleship design on the General Board of the United States Navy. This gave line officers and planners direct input and control over warship design, a pattern which has persisted to the present day.

Effects on fleet operations

Experience gained by the cruise led to improvements in formation steaming, coal economy and morale. Gunnery exercises doubled the fleet's accuracy. However, the mission also underlined the fleet's dependence on foreign colliers and the need for coaling stations and auxiliary ships for coaling and resupply.

Native Huts in the Village of Taboga, Taboga Island, Republic of Panama.

Calle del Frente, Colon, tomada de Cristobal, mostrando el comisariato de la compañia del Ferrocarril de Panama.

Front St., Colon, taken from Cristobal, showing Panama Railroad Commissary.

Vista reciente de Cristobal, Zona del Canal, mostrando oficinas de agencias de vapores, construidas de hormigon.

General View of Cristobal, Canal Zone, showing Concrete Steamship Offices.

Planta carbonera terminal del Atlantico, la mas grande del mundo en su clase, Cristobal, Zona del Canal.

Atlantic Terminal Coaling Plant, the largest of its kind in the World, Cristobal, Canal Zone.

Piers 7 and 8, Cristobal, Canal Zone.

www.ingramcontent.com/pod-product-compliance
Lightning Source LLC
Chambersburg PA
CBHW040033050426
42453CB00003B/100